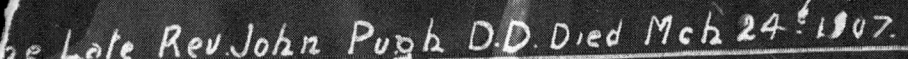
The Late Rev. John Pugh D.D. Died Mch 24th 1907.

© Day One Publications 2024

ISBN 978-1-84625-769-8

All Scripture quotations, unless stated otherwise, are from The Holy Bible, New King James Version Copyright © 1982 by Thomas Nelson, Inc. Used by Permission. All rights reserved.

British Library Cataloguing in Publication Data available

Published by Day One Publications
Ryelands Road, Leominster, HR6 8NZ
Telephone 01568 613 740
Toll Free 888 329 6630 (North America)
email—sales@dayone.co.uk
web site—www.dayone.co.uk

All rights reserved
No part of this publication may be reproduced, or stored in a retrieval system, or transmitted, in any form or by any means, mechanical, electronic, photocopying, recording or otherwise, without the prior permission of Day One Publications.

Frontispiece: Rev. John Pugh, D.D. (1844–1907)

Printed by 4edge Limited

Commendations

I welcome this thrilling new biography by Eryl Davies of one of the forgotten preachers to the unchurched people in the industrial areas of Wales. John Pugh worked tirelessly to bring the gospel to those in atrocious living conditions and who were affected by alcohol and sexual abuse. It is an informative and moving story that gives the honour to God for the hundreds of lives transformed. The author challenges readers in our contemporary world and includes practical encouragements for serving the Lord today.

Philip H. Eveson
Former Principal of the London Seminary

Breath-taking! Brace yourselves for what God can do through a man captivated by Christ's Calvary love. John Pugh was God's man with God's heart and vision to win Wales for Christ. This biographical gem is a must-read to reignite our hearts with love for Christ and people. While we are not all evangelists like Pugh, without every church member mobilised, he knew the unsaved masses would not be reached. He was also convinced that gospel work could not advance without 'Christ-possessed' women, which led to the full-time appointment of the 'Sisters of the People'. As you dive into this extraordinary work of God, see if you do not find yourself yearning for God to do it again and to use you!

Fiona Steward
Pastoral Worker (Women), Heath Church, Cardiff

This volume will be of interest and of hope to all those who pray for revival in Wales. It is a timely reminder of the power of the Holy Spirit working through those who give themselves absolutely to the Lord's calling to evangelise.

Dr Eryl Davies' account of the life and witness of John Pugh sets out clearly, through detailed descriptions of the progress made by the Forward Movement during those years leading into the 1904 revival, how the Lord called thousands to the assurance of salvation.

This story, presented with constant references to primary sources, is of critical relevance to all established denominations currently involved

Commendations

in arranging mission and church planting. It highlights both the human cost of living as an evangelist and the institutional tension that will be encountered as the work of the Spirit calls many to Christ in revival beyond the boundaries of established church life.

Dr Davies has undoubtedly provided us with a timely account of a largely forgotten period of the Lord's day of grace in Wales and how He raised John Pugh to be the eyes and heart of that day. We are indebted to Dr Davies for this work as it echoes the culmination of his own faithful ministry over the past fifty years and his constant prayer for the outpouring of God's Spirit in our day.

Rev. Aneurin Owen
Moderator, General Assembly of the Presbyterian Church of Wales

John Pugh was a man driven by his passionate love for Christ and for those Christ came to save. His story deserves to be told, not simply because it glorifies God but because it leaves today's Christian reader with an indelibly disturbing challenge. Well written and meticulously researched, here at last is a fitting tribute to another of Wales's greatly used heroes of the faith.

Rev. Jonathan Stephen
Former Principal, Union School of Theology

What a thrilling challenge it has been to read through this biography of John Pugh! The spiritual scene throughout Wales in his time was not dissimilar to that which we face today; the answer then and now is the same—to preach Christ in the power of the Spirit!

Pugh preached Christ with 'one arm clinging around the cross, and with the other outstretched to snatch souls from the wrath to come'! Pugh was also clearly not afraid to try new methods in attempting to reach the lost with the eternal gospel while maintaining the centrality of preaching.

I challenge anyone to read this account and remain unmoved to the great spiritual needs around us today; I thoroughly commend the book to you.

Rev. Andy Christofides
Assistant Pastor, Heath Church, Cardiff

Contents

COMMENDATIONS	3
PREFACE	6
1 MASSIVE CHANGES	9
2 1860 AND PEMBROKESHIRE	15
3 TREFECA COLLEGE	26
4 TREDEGAR: 1872–1881	31
5 PONTYPRIDD: 1881–1889	40
6 WIDER CONTACTS AND MINISTRY	48
7 CARDIFF: AN EPICENTRE	54
8 MORE GOSPEL ACTION AND SETH JOSHUA	62
9 'FELT MORE LIKE WEEPING'	77
10 'GRIT! GRACE! GUMPTION!'	89
11 AN EXPANDING WORK	101
12 '…IN LABOURS ABUNDANT…'	110
13 SCOTLAND AND WALES	120
14 THE FINAL DECADE	127
15 THE CLOSING MONTHS	138
16 JOHN PUGH AND HIS CRITICS	146
17 TENSIONS AND CHALLENGES	152
18 JOHN PUGH: THE LORD'S MESSENGER	159
19 WORD AND SPIRIT (1)	168
20 WORD AND SPIRIT (2)	174
21 CONTEMPORARY CHALLENGES	181

Preface

Having been ordained into the ministry of the Presbyterian Church of Wales, it has been a joy to write a biography of John Pugh who became a faithful gospel minister within the Presbyterian Church of Wales.[1] His achievements were enormous and thousands of people were influenced or saved through his ministry.

Originally my interest in John Pugh's ministry over the years was stimulated through personal contact with churches he established or helped to do so. In addition to one summer in Grove Chapel, Morriston, for two other successive summers I served as a student-pastor in Trinity Presbyterian Church, Nantyffyllon, Maesteg in the Llynfi Valley, a church which was pastorless. Coal mining was the dominant industry in the locality even in the 1960s and 1970s and Trinity Church was founded in the village by John Pugh in the late nineteenth-century[2] in order to reach the coal miners and their families with the gospel. Some of the older members of the church had heard stories of the beginning of the work and referred appreciatively to the labours of John Pugh in establishing the church, though they had never known anyone directly involved in that early period.

I have been familiar with other Forward Movement churches, especially in Cardiff like Saltmead, Memorial Hall and Heath,[3] to name only a few of the churches established by Pugh in the city, and also the Mission Hall in Neath. Currently I am a member and Elder in Heath Church, Cardiff, which has continued to exercise an influential ministry since a Hall was

---

1 Or its older name of Calvinistic Methodist.
2 'In Nantyffyllon, Maesteg, the Forward Movement is progressing very satisfactorily. The Rev. John Pugh conducted the services on Sunday 3 February 1895 and baptised seven children at the close of the evening service'—*The Monthly Treasury*, Vol. 2, No. 15, March 1895, p. 14.
3 See my book recounting blessing in these and other churches in the mid-twentieth-century: *Breeze From Heaven: Stories From Welsh Communities, 1940s–1980s* (Day One/Bryntirion Press, 2023).

Preface

first opened in November 1900 due to the initiative of John Pugh. The Rev. John Thomas had moved from his pastorate in Acrefair, Wrexham, to assist Pugh as his secretary and assistant in the Forward Movement, but in addition the Heath church members received him as their first official pastor on a part-time basis for a brief period.

After the main church building had been erected, on his death bed John Pugh asked the Rev. Francis Cole to become the pastor of Heath Church. Both Cole and the church members agreed and he became their minister in September 1907. Cole's ministry was signally blessed of the Lord and over the following decades the church grew and continues in the twenty-first century to minister to many people, young and old with a strong international mix.

I have other personal links with the Forward Movement. My late brother, the Rev. John M. Davies (1938–2019), became the pastor of the Forward Movement churches at Port Tennant and Burrows in the Docks area of Swansea in 1964. Pugh had developed a work here in what was regarded in the 1890s as 'one of the blackest spots in the area'. The work was difficult but fruitful in the 1960s. My brother's wife, too, Mrs Joan Davies (née Tolley) had been a Sister of the People in Newport before marriage, caring for a Forward Movement Centre on the Ringlands estate. Other Sisters of the People I have known included Mrs Morwen Higham and Mrs Joyce Akrill (née Dowber), the latter serving on the Gabalfa estate in Cardiff.

Alongside these personal links, however, this author has been challenged by Pugh's priorities, his deep love of Christ and zeal for the gospel.

This book focuses primarily on John Pugh and provides what is intended to be a popular introduction to his life and work. The book is not exhaustive and is in no way intended as a history of the Forward Movement. A more contemporary and thorough history of the Forward Movement is required, a history and analysis which will also need to track its sad demise. That story is complex, with the failure to build upon the work and priorities of John Pugh, but it is a story also reflecting the history and decline of the Presbyterian Church of Wales, doctrinally and numerically.

Preface

I pray this book will be used by the Lord to challenge and encourage Christians and churches in contemporary Britain and beyond in many countries. I long for us to witness again the gospel penetrating communities and vast groups of unchurched people in our localities, and bringing many people of all ages and backgrounds to trust in Christ.

To our triune God be all the glory now and for ever!

Eryl Davies
January 2024

Heath Church, Cardiff: Laying the Foundation Stones, 4th April 1906. This was also arranged as a 'welcome home' for Dr Pugh who for health reasons had travelled to Egypt and the Holy Land. He had only just returned, without any improvement in his health. Dr Pugh is in the centre. (This picture and the frontispiece were carefully and kindly photographed by Martin Forde from photographs hanging in the Minister's room of Heath Evangelical Church.)

1. Massive changes

The story of John Pugh is extremely relevant, even though he died more than a century ago in 1907. You may be surprised to read how challenging and strikingly contemporary his story is for Christians and churches in the twenty-first century.

One example is that in his ministry he faced desperate living and social conditions. Appalling poverty, homelessness, harsh living conditions especially in industrial areas, alcohol abuse, cruelty, immorality, and domestic as well as sexual abuse all confronted Pugh in his work on a daily basis. Constrained by the love of Christ, he endeavoured to help these men, women and children practically in different ways but without the limited regional or central government funding and resources available today.

Then there is the fact, like our own situation, that the majority of working-class people in industrial areas were unchurched and ignorant of the Christian gospel. Pugh's passion was to share with them the wonderful news that Christ had died for sinners and that they could become new persons in Christ. Pugh was neither 'professional' nor clinical in his dealings with these people. He loved them. He felt he had no choice but to work among them. Their practical and spiritual needs moved and distressed him; often he felt 'crushed in spirit' for them and their spiritual condition. However, the challenge does not end there. His own love of Christ was deep. Having himself been saved from a riotous way of life and brought by the Lord to experience the abundance of divine grace and forgiveness, he longed to see others enjoying Christ's love. Pugh had a great appreciation and awareness of what Christ had suffered for sinners at Calvary, so that he was delighted to love and share with people this good news about Christ. His story is uncomfortably relevant!

I feel privileged to share his story with you, and in the next chapter I will introduce you to the fourteen-year-old John Pugh who lived

Chapter 1

with his parents in Montgomeryshire, mid-Wales. The teenager later became well-known in Christian work in Wales, Scotland and even in South Africa.

Massive changes were afoot for John's family, but more especially for the nation as the industrial revolution gathered momentum in south-east Wales. Many living in the rural areas of Wales joined the drift of people from other parts of Britain and Ireland in moving to live and work in the developing industrialised areas of South Wales. Factories manufacturing tin and iron, together with the burgeoning coal industry, were in urgent need of labourers. The development of a rail network across Wales also attracted workers as the commercial benefits of the railway were quickly recognised by the new industries, especially for the transportation of coal but also facilitating travel for the population.

Several Christian businessmen in the vanguard of industrialisation in Wales influenced the Pugh family, but especially the son John, and I introduce them to you here because their names will occur in later chapters. Ezra Roberts was influential in the early period of Pugh's life in Pembrokeshire, and then David Davies with his son Edward were even more significant in progressing the industrial revolution in Wales in different ways, using their wealth generously to support Christian work. They both had a significant impact on John Pugh's life and contributed most in supporting him. There were also the Cory brothers, John and Richard, who were also good stewards of their wealth and encouraged Pugh personally as well as supporting his work.

David Davies (1818–90)

This man was 'one of the greatest entrepreneurs of nineteenth-century Wales'[1] and with John Cory[2] was a major player in the industrialisation of south-east Wales.

Davies became a wealthy industrialist who opened coal mines in the South Wales Valleys, employing as many as five thousand men in the

---

1 www.museum.wales
2 A ship-owner and broker, coal merchant and exporter as well as a coal owner who with his family supported Christian work liberally.

Massive changes

Rhondda alone, but only after he had developed significant parts of the railway system in Wales. He built most of the railway system in mid-Wales despite numerous engineering challenges. A major development for this man occurred in 1864 when he obtained a 'pioneer mineral lease' in the Rhondda valley to open mines to extract coal. Two years later the first pits were in full production. Five more coal mines were opened by 1886 before he created a new company, the Ocean Coal Company Ltd. In the wake of his success with coal, he became the driving force in the ambitious project of building Barry docks, near Cardiff. In the early period, Barry docks struggled to handle the vast amounts of coal being exported from Davies's coal-mines.

Although he became a wealthy businessman, his parents had been poor and worked a farm in the Llandinam area in Powys between Llanidloes and Newtown. He was the eldest of nine children and left school at the age of eleven to help his father on the farm while he developed skills in sawing timber for which he received commission.[3] When his father died in 1846, David was left to care for his younger brothers and sisters, but that same year he was invited to build the foundation and approaches for a bridge over the river Severn at Llandinam, and in this way his career as a contractor was launched. At the time of his marriage, he agreed to construct a railway between Llanidloes and Newtown which opened in 1859,[4] and in the process made 'a substantial profit'.[5] Importantly, David Davies became a Christian in his early years, actively supporting his local Calvinistic Methodist (Presbyterian) church in Llandinam and the Monthly Meetings for their churches in the region. He was recognised as a loyal Christian committed to Christian work in Wales and became part of the Lord's provision for John Pugh when he later pioneered evangelism in the industrial areas of South Wales. Davies also became an MP for the Cardigan area.

---

3 *Dictionary of Welsh Biography.*
4 Other railways he built were the Vale of Clwyd (1858), Oswestry–Newtown (1861), Newtown–Machynlleth (1862) , Pembroke–Tenby (1863) and an extension to Whitland (1866), then Pencader–Aberystwyth (1867).
5 *The Christian Standard*, Vol. 1. No. 5. November 1891.

Chapter 1

Edward Davies (1853–1898)

Edward was the only son of David Davies and inherited his father's vast estate. Edward Davies, like his father, was a Calvinistic Methodist. As a fluent Welsh speaker his church membership was in a Welsh language church, yet he recognised the urgent need in industrial areas to provide more English-language churches and services. He was the leading supporter of the Forward Movement and a personal friend of John Pugh, and became the first President of the First South Wales English Conference in 1884, then also of the second Conference a year later. His influence was considerable in commending and providing for the work of evangelism to which Pugh was committed. After his early death, his children continued their support of the Forward Movement. We will refer to him in more detail later in the book.

The Cory brothers

Brothers John (1828–1910) and Richard (1830–1914) were both ship and coal owners who had also committed themselves personally to Christ. John was a Wesleyan Methodist and Richard a Baptist, but they supported extensively the varied evangelistic work being undertaken across the denominations in Wales, support which included the Salvation Army. Pugh describes how he first met John Cory:

> John Cory invited us to spend the last evening of 1891 in his beautiful home. He invited us to place our scheme to evangelise the masses before him. Our simple but practical scheme so commended itself to his clear head and warm heart, that he there and then promised us his generous support.[6]

John Cory became a good friend and generous supporter of Pugh's work from this time. Cory's heart was very much in the work of the Forward Movement. In leading a re-opening service at Trehill Presbyterian Church three years earlier in 1898, Cory had challenged the congregation to action:

---

6 *Romance of the Forward Movement*, p. 85.

Massive changes

I would remind you, my fellow believers, that the church of God exists not only for your own spiritual benefit but also for the salvation of souls; and it is the good will and purpose of the Head of the Church that you men and women ... should have a hand, a share, in the blessed work of the salvation of others. It is God's divine purpose that in saving you, you should all become the saviours of others.

Ezra Roberts

Although lesser known and dying at the age of forty-one, the influence of Ezra Roberts on the teenage John Pugh was significant in earlier years, especially in helping provide preachers and encouraging John and other railway workers in Pembrokeshire to listen to gospel preachers. A native of St Asaph in North Wales, Ezra Roberts was another committed Christian, church member and a deacon while still a young man. He did whatever he could to spread Christ's gospel and support churches. He too was active in the Calvinistic Methodist Monthly Meetings for churches in the region and was highly respected.

Moving with his family to Pembrokeshire in 1861 to oversee with David Davies the building of the Pembroke–Tenby railway, Roberts enthusiastically supported evangelism and the planting of Calvinistic Methodist churches in the county. From 1863 he and his family were called to lay foundation stones for new chapel buildings in Pembroke Dock, Pembroke, Bethesda, Begelly and Saundersfoot. He contributed generously in support of the chapels and their pastors. What is of immediate interest for our story is that Roberts helped in arranging for chaplains to preach to the men working on the new railway and the teenage John Pugh benefited enormously from this provision which was a major factor leading to his conversion. Roberts's involvement with this railway ended a short time before his death in 1869. He had planned to return to North Wales with his wife and eight children to farm land at Bwlch in Cerigydrudion. His early death was a huge loss to the family and to churches.[7]

With this background in mind, we are ready to begin relating the story of the young John Pugh. The story, however, is more about the triune

---

7 *The Treasury*, Vol. 2, January 1870, pp. 23–27.

Chapter 1

God, Father, Son and Holy Spirit, whom John came to know, love and serve—sacrificially too. You will be surprised later by his love for Christ, but also his love for those who were not Christians and in desperate personal and social need! He was God's man in God's time for desperately needy sinners in industrial areas, many of whom were unchurched and addicted to alcohol, violence and infidelity. As a consequence, many of the working classes in these industrialised area became poorer and poorer. Their social needs were desperate but they also needed to hear about, and taste, the amazing love and grace of God in Christ.

John Pugh was God's man for this desperate situation. You can now read how he became a Christian and the ways he was used by the Lord.

2. 1860 and Pembrokeshire

An important year in the life of the Pugh family was 1860. This was the year the family moved to live in Pembrokeshire, south-west Wales. Their fourteen-year-old son, John Pugh,[1] had lived from birth with his parents in the same family house, Sunnyside, in the small village of New Mills in Montgomeryshire, mid-Wales. The prospect of relocation was probably more exciting than daunting for the teenager, for there was the prospect of working for his father. New Mills was a rural village in the attractive valley of the Afon Rhiw, a tributary of the River Severn and located close to the Wales/England border. Both parents, widely respected in the community, were strong Christians and faithful members of Beulah[2] Calvinistic Methodist church (Presbyterian) which was only a few yards from their home. Leaving Beulah would not have been easy for the parents, for John and Ann Pugh had relatives in the area and close church friends. To add to their pain in leaving, their small church had known considerable blessing in its brief history, with well-known preachers ministering there at regular intervals. John's mother Ann, was known for her godly life and zeal for the Lord, while his father John was a strong Christian who embraced Calvinistic theology,[3] nurturing his son in that God-centred faith.

Only six miles from New Mills was Pontrobert where the famous Rev. John Hughes (1775–1854) had been pastor. Hughes was a powerful preacher gifted in Greek and Hebrew, author of several biographies, articles, books and Welsh language hymns. His preaching was rich, powerful and widely influential. Unsurprisingly, Hughes was recognised

---

1 He was born in New Mills on 29th January, 1846.
2 Beulah was built in 1823 and rebuilt in 1882.
3 At the heart of this theology is the sovereignty of the triune God in creation, providence and salvation. The Welsh Calvinistic Methodist Confession of Faith of 1823 was binding on all their churches at least in this period.

Chapter 2

as one of the leaders of Calvinistic Methodism in that period in Wales. Ann Pugh's father, himself gifted in expounding Scripture, was related to John Hughes, so the Pugh family would have met John Hughes on occasions and heard him preach. Interestingly, Hughes's wife Ruth had been the maidservant of the famous Welsh hymn writer Ann Griffiths (1776–1805) at her home nearby in Dolwar Fach in Llanfihangel yng Ngwynfa. Ann had married a local farmer in October 1804 but died in August 1805 aged thirty following the birth of her child. Ann's profound hymns describing the love of God were preserved because she sang and recited them at home, and her maid Ruth had remembered them. John Hughes was also Ann Griffiths's minister for the last five years of her life, and he wrote the hymns down in two notebooks as his wife Ruth sang them from memory.[4]

John Pugh's mother must have shared this fascinating background with her son. The young boy would have met his famous uncle, Rev. John Hughes before he died, but the close proximity of Pontrobert to New Mills strongly suggests that John Pugh was influenced in some degree by this rich heritage in which the Bible and experiential Christianity were central. To what extent John benefited spiritually from church life in Beulah is uncertain, but both parents encouraged and nurtured him in understanding the gospel and before the age of fourteen he became a member of Beulah church.[5]

Although the church services were conducted in the Welsh language in Beulah, English was becoming dominant on the street and in school, so the teenage son was bilingual, equipped to cope with both languages in Pembrokeshire.

Before leaving for Pembrokeshire, one aunt asked John a question which suggests she herself had a personal faith in Christ: 'Will you

---

4   For the purpose of publication. John Hughes may have given the notebooks to Thomas Charles, Bala although Robert Jones, Rhos-lan, may have prepared them.
5   *Atgofion am John Pugh*, Annie Pugh Williams (Mrs W. Watkin Williams) (Gwasg Gomer, Llandysil. n.d.). The claim is made here that on becoming a member in New Mills before reaching the age of fourteen, John celebrated the occasion by holding open-air meetings among his neighbours.

1860 and Pembrokeshire

promise to read the Bible every day?' John had no hesitation in making the promise.

Why move to Pembrokeshire? The young John Pugh may not have realised how mobile the population in rural Wales was becoming, with some men with (or initially without) their families moving into South Wales, especially the counties of Glamorgan and Monmouthshire. People also came to South Wales from parts of England and Ireland. The attraction was the prospect of work with better wages, as iron factories, coal mines and even railways began to be built and expanded. John's father was a mason and there was the prospect of a long-term business contract in Pembrokeshire.

Only a year earlier the Pembroke and Tenby Railway Company had been formed by business people and local supporters who almost immediately received authorisation by Parliament (1859) to build a standard gauge railway line between Tenby and Pembroke Dock. This railway line began to be used in 1863, with an extension built between Tenby and Whitland by 1866. It is almost certain that John Pugh senior, a mason by trade, was recruited by two Christian businessmen, David Davies and business partner Ezra Roberts, tasked with building this railway. John Pugh's contract was to build bridges in strategic places over the railway. The fact that both businessmen were strong Christians and members within the Calvinistic Methodist Church would have appealed to John Pugh senior who had probably met them through Monthly District Meetings and quarterly Association meetings in the north. Having obtained the contract for building bridges over the railway between Pembroke Dock and Tenby, it was necessary for the Pugh family to move south. Their choice was to live in Tenby in close proximity to the railway station.

The teenager began working for his father immediately by helping in the office, work which brought him into close contact with the labourers or 'navvies' involved in building the railway. These men were rough and ungodly, spending leisure time and money in local taverns, drinking and often fighting. In this formative period of his life John joined them regularly, and one of his favourite habits was to buy drinks for some of the older women present so that he and others could laugh at their

John Pugh

Chapter 2

behaviour when they became drunk. Later he deeply regretted having done this.

Despite throwing himself into this riotous way of drinking and fighting with the railway workers, the Lord was dealing with him in various ways as relatives and friends continued praying for him.

John honoured the promise he had made to his aunt to read the Bible daily. One day he was reading Genesis chapter thirty-nine and was deeply challenged by the story of Joseph when he was tempted by his employer's wife to sleep with her while there were no others in the house. Joseph's response explains why he had to refuse: 'How then can I do this great wickedness, and sin against God?' Joseph repeatedly refused the woman's temptation, but when on one occasion she grabbed him he ran out of the house, only for her then to lie about him. John Pugh was convicted by Joseph's response to the married woman and soon his own lifestyle would change.

The Lord worked in further ways in his life, too, including the preaching and friendship of two students training for the Christian ministry and, in addition, the reading of a sermon in a monthly Christian Magazine. Prayers were now going to be answered!

Answered prayer

Ezra Roberts, in his concern for the gospel and those working on the railway line in Pembrokeshire, encouraged some young students training for the Christian ministry of the Calvinistic Methodist (Presbyterian) church to stay in the Tenby area during their summer vacations in order to engage in preaching and to care spiritually for the labourers building the railway line between Pembroke and Tenby. This was viewed as a mission to these railway labourers in the area and clearly it was visionary and necessary.

One of the students invited was **Thomas Charles Edwards** (1837–1900) who was studying in Lincoln College, Oxford. He went to Tenby for the summer weeks each year between 1863 and 1869. He was the great-grandson of Thomas Charles of Bala (1755–1814)[6] who had been an

---

6 For a popular biography read *No Difficulties with God: The Life of Thomas Charles, Bala (1755–1814)*, D. Eryl Davies (Fearn, Ross-shire, Christian Focus, 2022).

outstanding leader of the Calvinistic Methodist churches in that period. Edwards would have an illustrious career as a preacher, but also as the first Principal of the University College in Aberystwyth and later the second Principal of the Bala College where future ministers of the denomination were trained.

As a student, Edwards had been influenced profoundly in the 1859–60 revival in Wales to which Martyn Lloyd-Jones refers.[7] Home on vacation, he decided to attend a preaching meeting in Bala where the Rev. David Morgan—so greatly used in the revival—and a colleague were the preachers. Edwards was confused by the philosophy he was being taught in Oxford, so that he had serious doubts concerning the Christian faith. Lloyd-Jones claims that he attended the meeting more out of curiosity than anything else in order to hear what they were preaching. Unexpectedly, Edwards was dealt with profoundly under the preaching of the gospel as he sat in the gallery that day. He was changed, with his doubts vanishing as he saw the glory and perfection of Christ's work for sinners.

Edwards explains what happened on that occasion:

Here came two plain men to Bala and preached Christ simply, without fuss, without much else or eloquence, but they had more. Eternity came into the service; Heaven came into the place. The change I experienced was sufficient evidence to me of the divinity of Christianity. I was previously a lump of damnation and in that service I became a new creature.[8]

Consequently Edwards was full of passion and zeal for Christ and became an excellent preacher. As a student he was eager to evangelise the railway workers or 'navvies' as they were referred to in Pembrokeshire. John Pugh junior began to forge a warm relationship with this student and gained his personal support in future years for his ministry in reaching the needy working classes of people in the industrial areas of South Wales.

---

7 *Preaching and Preachers*, D. Martyn Lloyd-Jones (London, Hodder and Stoughton, 1971), pp. 322–323.
8 Quoted in Beautiful Feet: romans1015@outlook.com>1859-Welsh

Chapter 2

Another student was **David Lloyd Jones** (1843–1905), the son of a famous Calvinistic Methodist preacher in North Wales, John Jones, Talsarn (1796–1857). The Pugh family held his father in great esteem and had probably heard him preach on more than one occasion. David was a student in Edinburgh and, like Edwards, he too was powerfully affected by the 1859–60 revival in Wales. He became a popular preacher among the Calvinistic Methodists throughout Wales. Whenever David preached in Pembrokeshire during this period, John's parents were always in the congregation, either at Begelly (north of Tenby) or at Saundersfoot Calvinistic Methodist churches.[9] It was these two students in their friendship and preaching in the summer vacations who were used in speaking to the young teenager of his need of Christ.

There was, however, one other providential way in which John Pugh was dealt with in mercy by the Lord. One Sunday, the weather in Pembrokeshire was stormy and wet, and so the family decided to stay home on the Sunday rather than travel several miles to Bethesda, Saundersfoot, or Begelly. John's mother, Ann, gave him the latest issue of the Calvinistic Methodist monthly journal, Y *Drysorfa*,[10] to read. The journal was interesting with its varied articles, including news and feature columns, and the young John read the October 1866 issue. He enjoyed reading the varied content, but it was the sermon that attracted him and spoke powerfully to him concerning the glory of Christ and his own personal need of salvation. The sermon was by the Rev. William Charles (1817–1849) who hailed from Gwalchmai in Anglesey. A young preacher, he had endeared himself to congregations because of the quality and power of his preaching which was always full of Christ. Sadly he died

---

9 The Calvinistic Methodist Church was not established in Tenby until 1869.

10 Y *Drysorfa* (*The Treasury*) was first published as a monthly periodical in 1819 but ceased publication in 1823, later reappearing in 1831 as a quarterly. Early editors included Thomas Jones, Denbigh, and Thomas Charles, Bala. Under the editorship of John Parry it became a monthly journal with its final edition appearing in 1968. The journal included sermons, doctrinal articles, feature columns, correspondence from missionaries, reports of churches and denominational affairs. Poems and other literary works were included and Y *Drysorfa* became the first periodical to serialise the early works of Daniel Owen, including his novel *Rhys Lewis*. This was a paper enjoyed regularly by people in the many Calvinistic Methodist churches throughout Wales and in parts of England like Merseyside and London.

at the age of thirty-one from tuberculosis, but congregations continued to talk about his preaching years after his death.

The sermon was from Revelation 1:17–18:

And when I saw Him, I fell at His feet as dead. But He laid His right hand on me, saying to me, 'Do not be afraid; I am the First and the Last. I am He who lives, and was dead, and behold, I am alive forevermore. Amen. And I have the keys of Hades and of Death.'

Williams described briefly the remarkable revelation of the exalted Lord Jesus Christ given to the aged apostle John who was exiled on the Isle of Patmos for being a Christian and church leader. Conditions there were harsh and he would have been involved in slave labour despite being old and in his nineties. The sight of the Lord Jesus had a remarkable effect on John who fell at His feet as if he was dead. Being reassured by the Lord, he heard words that comforted him: *'I am the First and the Last'* indicating He is an infinite Saviour in charge of the universe He created and sustains, continuing to do so until the end of the world. And yet, John also hears Him say, *'I am He who lives, and was dead…'*. Now, said the preacher, the Lord is getting closer to John for John had seen Him suffering and dying on the cross and he was also a witness to His resurrection. Jesus died willingly and in love for sinners and conquered death, sin, hell and the devil: *'and behold, I am alive forevermore'*. Williams imagines he heard John shouting 'Amen', for this was enough to lift and encourage himself and the churches under persecution. The preacher again imagines the Lord responding—'But John, let Me tell you even more'—*'I have the keys of Hades and of Death'* with absolute authority and power over death and the destiny of people beyond the grave!

In his application, the preacher reminded the congregation that the Lord Jesus had fulfilled all the Old Testament expectations, promises, prophecies and types in dying on the cross for sinners. Williams then imagined the Lord standing on the edge of the ages and shouting: *'and was dead'* so that no more altars or sacrifices will ever be required again from sinners to appease the wrath of God. For that reason, Williams

Chapter 2

emphasised that Christ in His death had fulfilled all the conditions of peace with God and also provided a defence for all believers: *'Who is he who condemns? It is Christ who died, and furthermore is also risen...'* (Romans 8:34). The Prince is *'alive forevermore'* and victorious. These glorious facts, announced the preacher, should encourage sinners to come to Christ in faith, however much they have sinned and no matter how guilty they feel, for the Lord Jesus has died in the place of guilty sinners. Williams closed his sermon with a moving appeal: 'O sinner, bring your case to Him and trust Him.' At the same time he encouraged believers never to despair, for Christ lives to comfort them as pilgrims on their journey to heaven. Yes, 'Christ lives!'

As the young man read and pondered carefully over this sermon, he became aware of the holy, majestic character of God which resulted in a deep conviction and awareness of his personal sin, unworthiness and guilt before God. One biographer describes what happened:

As he began to read, the truth began to lay an increasingly strong hold on him. He began to tremble and shake ... he felt he was caught by a summons from above. He saw himself as a guilty creature before God and he was forced to his knees to beg for forgiveness. Here he was at last, his feet free from the fetters, a new creation in Christ.[11]

New values

One of the immediate actions on John's part following conversion was to forsake alcohol, so he signed the 'pledge' which the Temperance Movement provided and encouraged people to sign. That was not all. In repentance, feeling guilty for the time and money he had wasted on drink, John went even further. He visited the older women he had bought alcohol for in previous years in the taverns which resulted in their drunken behaviour, amusing both him and the other men. He begged their forgiveness and actually prayed with them and for them. He now had a new direction and values in life as a Christian. His life was changed.

---

11 Quoted by Geraint Fielder in his *Grace, Grit & Gumption: Spiritual Revival in South Wales* (Fearn/ Ross-shire/ Bridgend, Christian Focus/Bryntirion Press, 2000), p. 16.

1860 and Pembrokeshire

During this period in Pembrokeshire, even before his conversion, John had always attended the weekly services at Begelly, as well as the Sunday School, where he heard the Word taught faithfully. He had also appreciated the preaching of the students, Thomas Charles Edwards and David Lloyd Jones. During their summer vacational mission to Tenby and area to evangelise the railway workers, they were instrumental in reminding John of the gospel and preparing him, without his realising, for conversion. Their friendship was influential in many ways and important to John, friendships which continued over the years, providing support and encouragement for John's ministry and evangelism. Years later, John wrote an obituary for David Lloyd Jones and his influence on him in the early period:

I well remember his visit to take temporary charge of the navvies' mission in the absence of the late Dr Thomas Charles Edwards over forty years ago. Though I was not a professing Christian, yet the deep impression he left upon me and others was indelible. He preached a series of sermons on 'The prophecy of Balaam', 'The Root of Jesse', and 'The Star of Jacob'. My parents and others who almost worshipped his renowned father were delighted with his young and promising son, and they prophesied that he would prove a worthy successor of his father, the immortal John Jones, Talsarn. I never missed one of his sermons, and I had the privilege of hearing him deliver his first English sermon in Bethesda Chapel, Tenby; and I well remember his nervousness and his telling my father: 'I must act the parson tonight and read my sermon.'[12]

The influence of both David Lloyd Jones and Thomas Charles Edwards therefore was incalculable on John's life and he remained aware throughout his life of his spiritual indebtedness to them. He admired their preaching ministries over the years and their invaluable support later.

Following his conversion, he formally entered into membership of Zion Calvinistic Methodist (Presbyterian) Church in Begelly where he

---

12 *The Romance of the Forward Movement of the Presbyterian Church of Wales*, Rev. Howell Williams. This was the Davies Lecture given at the General Assembly of the Presbyterian Church of Wales in Aberaeron, June 1946 (no publishing date), pp. 26–27.

Chapter 2

was warmly welcomed and nurtured. Zion church had been established in 1828 to minister to the colliers in the area. During 1849 in what is referred to as the Cholera revival, the work grew considerably and a gallery was added to the building to accommodate the numbers of people attending. Again in the early 1860s[13] the church was affected for good by another revival which the Pugh family either experienced directly, or were made to feel the impact of the Spirit's powerful work in the church which the family attended.

Love for Christ

John quickly recognised the importance of the local church where the Word of God is preached and honoured, and so he committed himself wholeheartedly to Christ and His church. The pastor of Begelly church was the Rev. George Bancroft (1841–1899), who hailed from England. He had himself moved to live in Swansea with a relative and while there attended the Presbyterian church in Argyle where the pastor, the Rev. William Williams, helped him considerably. Bancroft was only five years older than John but he recognised in the latter huge potential and proceeded to disciple and befriend him, lending him books to read while always seeking his spiritual development. There were other Calvinistic Methodist ministers who recognised the young man's potential. For example, the first minister of the recently established church in Tenby (1869) the Rev. John Davies and the elderly Rev. William Powell (1818–1894), Westgate Church, Pembroke, also encouraged the young Pugh, particularly regarding his awareness of a divine 'call' to the Christian ministry and then supporting him when he applied to enter Trefeca College for training in 1869.

From the moment of his conversion, John became excited over the gospel of Christ, recognising the spiritual and moral needs of people to receive grace and forgiveness in Christ. This love for Christ was like a fire within him, constraining him to share the gospel with others. Almost immediately he gathered around him a small group of young people who

---

13 Zion church, Begelly was rebuilt in 1866. For the opening of the new building a special train brought crowds of people from Tenby to attend the meetings. Seven sermons were preached on that occasion!

shared his love for Christ and began a series of open-air preaching meetings in the Tenby area. His leadership qualities which began to emerge, as well as his gift of preaching and a deep love for people, would be used in remarkable, even unusual ways, in the future.

Following his conversion and dominating his life was his personal commitment to Christ coupled with a deep appreciation of God's love in Christ. The substitutionary death of Christ on the cross for sinners meant everything to him, together with His resurrection, ascension and session at the right hand of the Father in heaven where He exercises absolute authority and power over all. As a consequence, he possessed a deep love for people and longed for them to know the Saviour and His saving grace.

But what did the Lord want him to do with his life? Although enjoying a comfortable job and a good salary, he became aware of the Lord calling him to become an ordained preacher and pastor. His response was prayed over for a period of time which involved him in long periods of personal prayer for guidance and assurance. He sought advice from respected pastors and valued their encouragement. The local church at Begelly encouraged him wisely in this direction and eventually he applied for training in Trefeca College where the Rev. William Howells was Principal. There were hurdles to face before entering College, like the Ministerial Monthly Meeting examination which he passed. Then he was accepted as a member of the Pembrokeshire Monthly Meeting, which all church elders and ministers were expected to attend. His suitability as a potential pastor had been considered carefully by pastors and the denominational structures had also involved careful assessment.

At the age of twenty-three, nine years after relocating with his parents to Pembrokeshire, John Pugh entered Trefeca College in the Autumn of 1869 to train for the ministry of the Calvinistic Methodist Church, which increasingly became known as the Presbyterian Church of Wales.

3. Trefeca College

Trefeca! The name was well known in Wales, even into the twentieth-century despite the fact that Trefeca was originally only a hamlet in the parish of Talgarth.

Trefeca is located between Talgarth and Llangorse Lake in south Powys, eight miles south of Hay-on-Wye. What made Trefeca famous was that Howel Harris (1714–1773), one of the leaders in the early period of Calvinistic Methodism in Wales, had been born there, and made Trefeca his base for his work. He constructed a building there to accommodate a community of people with the Countess of Huntingdon also establishing a Theological Seminary there in 1768 to train preachers under Harris's watchful eye. Among the students who enrolled in that first year were six students expelled from St Edmund Hall, Oxford due to their 'Methodist' sympathies. By 1792 this training College was transferred to Cheshunt in Hertfordshire, while Thomas Charles (1745–1814) was eager to adopt the Trefeca College for training purposes. However, the Bala revival of 1792 and other demands on his time meant he was unable to pursue the venture. Eventually, in 1842, the Calvinistic Methodist Association of churches[1] in South Wales opened Trefeca as their College to train future ministers and the Rev. David Charles served as the first Principal from 1842 to 1863.

College

One can only imagine the excitement in the autumn of 1869 when the twenty-three year old John Pugh went as a candidate for the Christian ministry to Trefeca College in order to pursue a rigorous three-year course of study. The Principal was the Rev. William Howells (1818–1888), a man who deserves mention, for the young Pugh respected him greatly.

---

1 The Bala College was opened in 1837 to train men from both North and South Wales for the Christian ministry of Calvinistic Methodist churches. From 1842 therefore men from South Wales were re-directed to Trefeca rather than Bala for their training.

Trefeca College

Howells was born and educated in Cowbridge in South Wales before becoming an apprentice at the age of fourteen to an ironmonger. Later, aware of a divine call to become a church minister and preacher, he trained in the Countess of Huntingdon's College in Cheshunt in Hertfordshire before becoming one of the first students to train in Trefeca when it opened in 1842 for men from South Wales. He completed his studies there in 1845 and then for a period of twenty years pastored three churches.[2] Not only did he have a pastoral heart but he was an excellent teacher and 'an exceptionally acceptable preacher'. Despite his gifts, Howells was a humble and unassuming man, confining most of his preaching to small English churches and avoiding publicity. 'It is probable that Wales never had as great a preacher who was known to so few people.'[3] He retired from the College in 1888 and died later that year.

How did the students regard John Pugh? One fellow-student, Rev. John Hughes, Liverpool, later offered several insights concerning Pugh as a student. He was physically attractive with an athletic figure, always a cheerful and generous man who often broke out into 'peals of laughter'. Hughes describes him as 'the most distinguished of students for personality and presence' although not destined to be a great scholar or original in the area of theology. At the same time, Hughes adds, Pugh 'ever continued to be the real evangelist with obvious popular gifts which eminently qualified him for the work of his life. He was raised to be the great evangelist of our church; nor do I think that a greater one was given to any church'.[4]

Pugh was conscientious in his studies, reading the required text-books and enjoyed attending lectures; he also enjoyed College life and developed friendships with students and Professors, some of which continued throughout his life. However, Pugh remained *par excellence* an evangelist preacher' and the following incident in College illustrates his passion for gospel preaching. Each Saturday morning during the College term, it was the custom for a student to preach a sermon in front of all the students and the Principal who then invited observations and criticisms from the

---
[2] Swansea (1845–51), Zion, Carmarthen (1851–57) and Windsor Street, Liverpool (1857–65).
[3] *Dictionary of Welsh Biography.*
[4] *The Romance of the Forward Movement*, p. 30.

Chapter 3

students. This was a difficult experience for students, but on this occasion, after the sermon had been preached, there was applause from the class. The Principal then commented that 'there are some discourses we have listened to in this place which ... are hardly worth passing an opinion upon. But the sermon we have just heard not only invites criticism but seems to provoke it', and he then urged the students to feel free in passing their own judgements on the sermon. A number of students praised the sermon for its style, elegance, exegesis and its language, then the Principal turned to Pugh, explaining, 'We expect an opinion from you.' Pugh's response was honest, revealing his passion for evangelism:

'Well, sir', he responded, 'I agree with much that is said in favour of the sermon we have heard. The diction was polished and the periods well rounded and all that; but I hope our brother is not going to preach that sermon to any congregation for it has one fatal defect—it will never save a single soul!'

Pugh did not complete his third year of studies in Trefeca because several churches were keen to consider him as their potential pastor in North and South Wales. He had become a popular preacher, and being bilingual he had been able to preach in both English- and Welsh-speaking churches with the result that he was in demand. College studies had not dampened any of his fervour and passion for preaching the gospel and he could not wait to commence his life's work of ministry. Despite the interest of several churches in him, he was acutely aware of the masses of working class people and their families living in the new industrial areas of South Wales. Here was a mission-field close to his heart. The unfolding story relates how the Lord led him to a church, and it was a church so clearly planned by the Lord. We refer to this guidance as providence.

Providence

While Pugh had been studying in Trefeca College, the mobility of people moving to South Wales in search of employment continued apace and this was true of men leaving rural Pembrokeshire. One example illustrates the Lord's providence for the young Pugh. Four Badham brothers—John,

Trefeca College

Benjamin, William and Richard—were members of Begelly Calvinistic Methodist church and knew John Pugh junior well. They had known him before his conversion and were aware of his lifestyle in the taverns while also attending preaching meetings in their church on Sundays. They had been thrilled to hear of Pugh's conversion and then membership in their church at Begelly. During Pugh's period of study in Trefeca, the four Badham brothers decided to move from their family home to work in Tredegar. This was a huge change for them, but they were believers and immediately joined a small church with only sixteen members that was traditional and faithful to God's Word. The church had been established about 1867 when a few keen Christians gathered for Bible study. They then used a bakery as a meeting place before taking over a small corrugated iron building situated on a cinder tip, known as the Tin Chapel, where a church was formed with fewer than ten members. By 1872 there were sixteen members and the small chapel was half-full on Sunday evenings for their worship service. The members of the Tin Chapel had made little, if any, impact on the community and no corporate attempts were made to share the gospel with others in the town.

During his third year of studies in Trefeca, and despite invitations from other churches to become their pastor, John Pugh felt in his heart a deep desire to evangelise in needy industrial areas of South Wales. In a prayerful attitude, the members were considering calling someone to be their pastor, but the thoughts of the Badham brothers turned naturally to John Pugh. When it was agreed that the Badham brothers approach him to consider becoming the pastor of the Tin Chapel, Tredegar, the young student felt sure of God's leading in the matter. He was thrilled at the prospect of preaching to people in an area where there was great spiritual need. Convinced that the Lord was leading him in this direction, he decided to end his studies in Trefeca a little earlier in his third year in order to become the first pastor of Tin Chapel. In an unrelated providence, John's parents had also moved from Pembrokeshire to Nantymoel in the Ogmore valley of Glamorgan where his father had the task of building the Ocean colliery but also erecting houses for colliery workers to live in with their families.

Chapter 3

On the first Sunday of July 1872, John Pugh began his ministry with an annual salary of £50. And now the Tin Chapel would begin to grow and impact the community.

That is the theme of the next chapter.

4. Tredegar: 1872–1881

John Pugh was a tall, handsome young man with a strong physique. He had a colourful, joyous and outgoing personality, often expressed in an infectious laugh and sense of humour which characterised his open-air preaching to great advantage. His voice was rich and powerful, ideal for outdoor speaking and preaching while he was also able to sing, as illustrated when he started open-air preaching in Tredegar. He was quick-witted, brave and full of initiative throughout his life. An extrovert with a positive attitude to life in general, yet for Pugh this was accompanied by a sensitive, compassionate attitude towards people. He never appeared sad or negative but often spontaneously and kindly encouraged others to trust and joy in the Lord rather than be downcast or in despair and unbelieving. He was a people's man with excellent interpersonal qualities.

What stands out about this man is that he cared for people, a fact quickly recognised by individuals and congregations. Warmth and love radiated from him so naturally when he spoke and preached. Essentially a man of action and a competent organiser, he found it difficult not to act when he observed pressing needs requiring an urgent response. His inevitable response to the needs of individuals and communities expressed a deep, heartfelt compassion. Such needs moved him to action, a fact which critics too often ignored. And in talking about such needs he would often weep in his appeal for support. Pugh loved the Lord and people deeply and longed to help them, practically and spiritually. An unselfish man, he was always prepared to forgo his own comforts to help others, whoever and wherever they were.

Settling

Settling into his first pastorate was eased by the care and support provided, especially by the four Badham brothers who encouraged him in his work

Chapter 4

but also ensured he relaxed with them. One of the sports they loved playing in the summer months was quoits, a favourite outdoor game in the mining area. Quoits involved the throwing of metal, rope or rubber rings over an agreed distance, usually to land over a spike or as near to it as possible. In daily life and in his work as pastor, his presence in the locality was soon felt as he made himself known to locals and started preaching in the Tin Chapel. Slowly the numbers of those attending began to increase and the small building was quickly filled on a Sunday evening.

There are at least five memorable details relating to his nine-year ministry in Tredegar which deserve mention.

One detail relates to the numerical growth of adherents and members at the Tin Chapel. The young pastor possessed excellent interpersonal gifts and loved being with people. He initiated conversations continually, he was approachable, and while serious-minded yet he was cheerful and often burst out in laughter at things which he or people said or did. He was a natural and people were drawn to him. John Pugh had a colourful personality, as the locals quickly discovered.

But he was a preacher who cared for the people and he preached in a language and at a level they understood and with a passion which gripped them. His message was Christ-centred and his aim in preaching Christ was to urge and plead with people to trust Christ. Always at the heart of his preaching was Christ crucified whose death for sinners was substitutionary, penal and effective in reconciling sinners to a holy God through the agency of the Holy Spirit and the instrumentality of personal faith in the person of Christ. His preaching was therefore direct, arresting and convicting.

No wonder then that people were being converted under his preaching, and the personal testimonies of converts in their families and among their work colleagues gave further publicity to the preaching of the new pastor at the Tin Chapel. Increasing numbers of new people were attracted to the church services and the small building would soon be too small to accommodate all the hearers. Numerical growth coupled with conversions should not blind us to the man himself, for he was not only in love with Christ and passionate about the gospel but a man who also prayed often, in dependence on the Holy Spirit to make the preaching effective in terms of conversions and spiritual growth. And the social as well as the spiritual conditions of people in the area further drove John Pugh to his knees pleading for the Lord's help and power in preaching. Prayers were certainly answered abundantly!

Town Clock

Secondly, despite the numerical and spiritual growth of the Tin Chapel, the young pastor was far from satisfied, for there were many thousands of needy and unconverted people in the immediate locality who desperately needed to hear the gospel. The need existing among the locals had gripped him. His heart went out to them in love and prayer. He was aware of a divine compulsion to preach the gospel to these people, wherever they were. The burden on his heart gave him no choice but to take urgent action to reach the unchurched. This note of urgency remained with him until his death.

Towards the end of his first month in Tredegar he shared with the church officers his plan to reach those who never attended gospel services. The friendly church officers did not oppose his plan, but neither did they offer to help or encourage him. It was likely he would preach outside without help from them or church members. On the last Sunday evening in July 1872, therefore, the pastor informed the church that at 7.00 pm on the following Tuesday evening he would be leading an open-air service at the Town Clock which was ideally located in the centre of the town. Those in the service that evening were invited to join him and stand alongside him for support and encouragement.

On that Tuesday evening, there were many discouragements. Pugh stood on the step below the clock and watched the people passing by, but there were no church officers or members to be seen. Holding his Welsh and English language New Testament which he referred to as his 'double-barrelled gun' and a hymn book, he was almost ready to start the service when he saw a few women from the church arrive and stand by his side. He was greatly encouraged by their presence and years later in ministry he often said: 'Never have I been disappointed by Christ-

Chapter 4

possessed women.'[1] The pastor then announced a hymn and urged the women to join him in the chorus. Having a strong baritone voice, he began to sing:

I hear Thy welcome voice,
That calls me, Lord, to Thee,
For cleansing in Thy precious blood
That flowed on Calvary.

The ladies joined him in the chorus:

I am coming, Lord,
Coming now to Thee;
Wash me, cleanse me in the blood
That flowed on Calvary.

This was a new hymn and had only been written earlier that same year in America by an American Methodist minister in Epworth, Iowa, whose name was Lewis Hartsough (1828–1919) who also wrote the music. The hymn was used often by Sankey in his mission meetings.[2] Pugh was well informed as to what was happening in other parts of the United Kingdom and was open to modern songs and tunes as well as methods of reaching unbelievers. All the new hymns/songs, however, had to express the gospel clearly. After singing the hymn, Pugh prayed, asking the Lord for His help. Pugh did not remember how long he prayed, but he added,

When I opened my eyes, after being on the mount with God, a great crowd of men and women stood before me gazing in amazement into my eyes.

---

1 *The Romance of the Forward Movement*, pp. 36–37.
2 This was literally a new hymn published in the revised edition of *The Revivalist* (1872) only weeks earlier. Sankey discovered the hymn in a monthly periodical, *Guide to Holiness* (1873) and described it as 'this beautiful hymn'. The hymn was included also in Sankey's Collection of Hymns (*Gospel Hymns*, No. 2, 1876 by Sankey & Philip P. Bliss) and in successive editions of *Sacred Songs and Solos*. .

He did not take a traditional approach by announcing a Bible text but started unexpectedly with a warning to all the people looking at him:

Boys, they tell me that you are an awful set here, and that you were in the habit of throwing rotten eggs at the head and mud into the mouth of a dear old minister who used to stand up here and tell you of Jesus and his love. I am not afraid of anyone in this crowd, but I am awfully afraid of myself, for if any of you should insult me and I lose my temper, I should surely mark that man.

There was an immediate response from the crowd. Pugh recalled the incident:

One fine, strong, toughish-looking collier in the crowd cried out: 'Go on youngster: I'll stand by you. The man who insults you will have to reckon with me.'

The young preacher was certainly glad of his support and the meeting went on without any insults or interference. The gospel had been preached to many local, unchurched folk. And they had listened. Among that crowd, some would be saved. Pugh was encouraged and relieved he had been enabled to preach outside to unbelievers.

Opposition

A third incident illustrates the discouragement and opposition Pugh experienced, but unexpectedly from his own denominational churches, regarding preaching in the open air. These established Welsh language churches in the area were conservative, traditional and becoming more respectable. They also tended to appeal more to the middle classes rather than to labourers and the unchurched. Some church elders referred to Pugh as a 'ranter', accusing him of bringing the denomination and even the gospel into disrepute. The charges were serious and troubling. But the Lord dealt with the opposition in an unusual way. One Sunday the Welsh language Presbyterian church whose officers were critical of Pugh had arranged for two well-known preachers to preach to their congregation. One of the preachers was the Rev. William Howells, Principal of Trefeca

Chapter 4

College, whom Pugh knew and respected from his period of studies there. The other preacher was the Rev. Edward Matthews, Ewenny, one of the outstanding preachers amongst the Calvinistic Methodists, and widely respected as an author. Both visiting preachers heard from the church officers of their criticisms of Pugh's open-air preaching and they decided to investigate for themselves. They suggested to Pugh that he should preach at the Town Clock that Sunday evening at 8.00 pm. Although far from being keen to do so on the Sunday evening, Pugh agreed to their request. Pugh himself relates what happened that evening:

As I was giving out the hymn, the great Edward Matthews arrives with all the Welsh church officers, 'There was an immense crowd of earnest listeners. As the Spirit of God moved upon that vast congregation, I could see the countenance of the dear old Principal lighting as though it were transfigured, and the wonderful eyes of Edward Matthews rolling in their sockets, and the tears flowing over his cheeks. At the close, Matthews came up to me, and putting his two hands upon my shoulder, he closed his eyes and said: 'God bless you, my boy. I am thankful that Howel Harris is not dead. I never felt myself such a big sinner as I am now, for had I and others done this in our life, Glamorganshire and Monmouthsire would not be in the grip of the evil one.'

At that point, the young preacher turned to Matthews, Ewenny, expressing surprise and disappointment:

But, Mr Matthews, the gentlemen who have accompanied you declare that I am not a Methodist, and that I am dragging the blessed gospel into the mire.

Matthews's response was immediate but reassuring:

It is you who are the true Methodist. This is Methodism. This is what made Welsh Wales what it is today; and this is what must transform Glamorganshire and Monmouthshire.[3]

---

3   *The Romance of the Forward Movement*, pp. 38–39.

Tredegar: 1872–1881

We are not informed what the two eminent preachers said to the church officers who had been critical of Pugh's open-air preaching. One thing is certain. The church officers changed their minds after witnessing the full approval given to Pugh by these two famous preachers and by being reminded of the early beginnings of Calvinistic Methodism in Wales under preachers like Howel Harris, Daniel Rowland and many others for whom preaching outdoors was practised extensively to reach people with the gospel. Pugh was only continuing in the tradition and zeal of these men of God. Those church officers who had criticised Pugh's preaching outside now became his staunch supporters. Pugh was greatly encouraged and as many as a thousand people met regularly around the Town Clock on Sunday evenings to hear him preach.

Problems of growth

Not only was Pugh now well-known in Tredegar but also in a wider area as reports of his work were made known. One major problem was that the Tin Chapel was far too small and inadequate to cope with the numbers of people being converted and unbelievers being drawn to the church services. Drastic and urgent action was required. They decided to rent the Temperance Hall which had a seating capacity for one thousand people. On Sunday evenings the hall was crowded, and mostly with young people eager to hear the preaching. Previously they had never attended a church but had been reached by the open-air preaching services. However, the Temperance Hall was only a temporary measure and a request was made to the Monmouthshire Monthly Meeting of the Calvinistic Methodists for permission to erect a large and permanent church building. Progress in considering the request was slow, but eventually, within four years, a large building accommodating seven hundred people was built. The builder, of course, was the pastor's own father who was now living and working in the area and was an experienced building contractor!

Marriage

The final detail we need to record is the pastor's marriage in 1875. In the Lord's providence once again, John Pugh was preaching one Sunday near

Chapter 4

Abergavenny in a church with the name of Moserah. Over the weekend he spent there, he met an attractive and godly young lady, Mary Watkins. For the young Pugh, it was love at first sight! As the girl's parents were informed of a likely romance, they had reservations concerning their daughter marrying a Calvinistic Methodist minister whose financial income would never be regarded as adequate by their standards. Her parents were successful farmers near Raglan and wanted security for their daughter rather than poverty and a hard life as a pastor's wife, albeit they had nothing personal against John Pugh and respected him.

In later years, Pugh's daughter by this marriage recorded her mother's memories of the objection to her parents marrying:

> I believe I heard my mother say that my grandparents did not look very favourably upon the attention which the young minister paid to their daughter. They prophesied an unhappy future for her if she paid little heed to what she would bring upon herself in marrying a Calvinistic Methodist minister. Her life would be one of hard labour and obscurity ... They explained they had no personal objections to young Mr Pugh, but marriages were not made in heaven but rather here on the hard soil of earth where income etc. needed careful consideration. In reply he had argued the promises of the Bible that 'all these things' would be added to those who sought first the kingdom of God and cast all their care upon Him.[4]

This difficulty was overcome, though the details are obscure, and Pugh courted Mary Watkins for a brief period before marrying on April 25th, 1875 in Sion Street Baptist Chapel, Abergavenny. The bride was twenty-five years old and the bridegroom four years older. Their marriage was a very happy one with both being committed to serving the Lord. Daughter Annie Pugh Williams describes her mother as being intellectually able with a strong character and an attractive personality. She was also kind and warm in her attitude towards people which was ideal for the kind of ministry her husband would be involved in. Her love of Christ was deep and expressed in many ways but particularly in loving those in social

---

4 *Atgofion am John Pugh*, 14; Grace, Grit and Gumption, pp. 22–23.

Tredegar: 1872–1881

and spiritual need in society. This woman shared her husband's burdens for the work of evangelism, sharing their joys together and sacrificial in fulfilling their ministry. The marriage was made in heaven, after all!

For six further years John and Mary Pugh served in Tredegar and witnessed the success of the gospel in many exciting ways. Hundreds of people were converted, and in the nine years of his pastorate in Tredegar the small number of sixteen members increased to well over four hundred. In the latter years he received several invitations to pastor other churches, but these were declined as his ministry in Tredegar had not yet ended. However, during his ninth year in the pastorate, he felt that God was calling him away to another challenging situation, namely to a small English language church in Pontypridd. He and his wife moved there in 1881. And in Pontypridd the story becomes more exciting.

We will resume the story in the next chapter!

5. Pontypridd: 1881–1889

The name 'Pontypridd' is rich in significance and history. Really! The Welsh word for bridge, for example, is 'Pont', and the rest of the name can be translated as 'earthen house'. Originally there were several wooden bridges spanning the river Taff which runs through the town and there was also a mud-bricked house located alongside the main wooden bridge crossing the river, so the name Pontypridd was very apt, being formally adopted in 1856. The two rivers, namely the Taff and the Rhondda, converge alongside this town.

Pontypridd is the 'gateway' to the two Rhondda Valleys which extend for sixteen miles north-west of the town. The Rhondda Valleys became heavily populated from the time of the industrial revolution when coal mines were built with coal becoming the dominant industry and employer in the latter part of the nineteenth century until its decline by the 1970s. Pontypridd was a convenient and necessary social and shopping centre for the Valley people, with the lucrative alcohol trade flourishing in the town and adding to the many social problems already existing.

Pontypridd also proved to be a 'gateway' in another way. When John Pugh began his ministry in the town in 1881 he began to exercise a powerful but more extensive ministry to the unchurched people in the area from 1881, and as a result he became more widely known in the region as well as in the country.

A challenge!

John Pugh accepted an invitation to become the minister of an English language Presbyterian church which did not have its own building but met in a church hall which could accommodate about three hundred people. The church was somewhat traditional, complacent and made only feeble efforts to reach the masses of unchurched people living in the town and others who socialised there often at weekends. Most of the

Pontypridd: 1881–1889

services in other chapels were exclusively Welsh-speaking which excluded a significant number of working-class people who had moved into the area for employment from Cornwall, Devon, Somerset, Herefordshire and further afield. These people would not have understood the Welsh language, so there was an additional challenge to reach them through the medium of English. Although some Welsh-speaking people moved into the area from rural areas of Wales, their commitment to Christianity and chapel life was variable. The challenge of reaching both Welsh- and English-speaking workers and their families was considerable, but too many churches failed to face up to the challenge.

Within a month of commencing his ministry in the town, and after walking often around the town, Pugh had identified an ideal place for open-air preaching. Near Pontypridd railway station, he became familiar with the 'square', referred to locally as 'The Tumble' which had as many as seventeen pubs within close proximity. He soon learned that those spending money and time drinking in the pubs referred to themselves as the Tumble Gang. This was a hostile area for folk to enter, but Pugh was thrilled because it would provide an ideal spot for preaching the gospel. He informed his church leaders that he intended to preach in that location on the Saturday evening, but there was no enthusiasm or support expressed by the church officers or members. He would be alone in the venture. By the time Saturday evening arrived and Pugh was ready to preach, no one from the church arrived to stand with him. He was disappointed, but his longing for people to hear of Christ constrained and motivated him again that evening.

Walking on his own, he was aware of twenty or more men in a group and discussing a fight that would take place. He interrupted the conversation but was told to leave. He ignored their order, then explained to them:

Men, I propose preaching on this spot this evening, but I don't see any saints about here to stand by me, only some poor sinners like myself—for I once belonged to your school—but I have given up knocking men about. I have taken to fighting the devil and his imps. Will you stand by me, for I am a stranger here?[1]

---

1 *The Romance of the Forward Movement*, pp. 42–43.

Chapter 5

They agreed to stand with him, and at Pugh's request they formed a ring around him. Pugh started by singing a Christian song, then preached. There were frequent touches of humour and ample illustrations in his address which connected with the men. They listened avidly to the preacher, then at the end he invited them to attend his service on Sunday evening:

> Some of you may not have Sunday clothes, for the slaves of the devil do not have such things ... but if you come to Christ He will give you a new heart and then will come the new clothes and the new furniture and the new home—'old things will pass away. I will make all things new'. But until these new things come, men, come to the Hall and come in time and take any vacant seat that you see and like, for we do not keep seats for any favourites or any big swell and his family.[2]

The emphasis by Pugh on 'any vacant seat' was breaking with a strong tradition developing in Welsh language chapels where the members had their seats reserved, especially if they were important families, and often the seats were paid for on a regular basis by worshippers. These people therefore paid for their seats in addition to any gifts they gave to the church. In a stroke, Pugh removed this hindrance to the poor attending a chapel service and welcomed anyone and everyone to sit where seats were vacant.

The open-air preaching meetings at The Tumble continued indefinitely and became extremely popular, being attended by many unchurched people. The inevitable opposition to Pugh's preaching was planned to disrupt and end his preaching there. Those organising the opposition were the owners of the seventeen pubs around The Tumble. On the first occasion they arranged for a drunken man to interfere with the service, but Pugh carried on as normal. Then they used a town crier and the ringing of a bell to spoil the service, but Pugh's loud, melodious voice won the day. A brass band was engaged by the pubs to drown the voice of the preacher. This appeared to work, but when the band needed to rest between playing tunes and gather their breath, Pugh immediately preached, taking advantage of their enforced rest. His policy was: 'When

---

2 *Grace, Grit & Gumption*, p. 25.

they got puffed, I preached'! The Lord used their opposition to increase the sympathy and support of local people for Pugh's ministry and his congregations increased in number continually.

Conversions and temperance

Significant numbers of men and women became Christians through Pugh's open-air preaching. Their lives were changed as they became committed to Christ and His church. Now the preacher had plenty of people to stand alongside him in the open-air services and to share their own testimony with friends and family. These new Christians turned their backs on alcohol and with their families they benefited by releasing more of their wages for food, clothing and more comfortable living conditions.

Converts were encouraged to wear a blue ribbon as an indication that they would totally abstain from drinking alcohol. This became known as the 'Blue Ribbon' campaign and in January 1882 a Temperance Mission was launched. Having seen the cruel consequences of alcohol abuse, especially in driving individuals and their families into dire poverty, Pugh was set against the alcohol business world and so a Temperance Mission was launched in the first month of 1882. Pugh was not unique in linking the Temperance Movement to evangelistic preaching, for during the previous decade this had become a new practice in England due to the impact of alcohol on the family and social lives of people. An American evangelist, D. L. Moody had also encouraged this development in his campaigns. While well-intentioned in attacking a major cause of poverty and cruelty, it became too closely aligned to the gospel of Christ, with some people becoming total abstainers yet without being born again and trusting in Christ. A future generation would be imbibed with a hatred of alcohol accompanied by a self-righteousness and a negative attitude towards the gospel of Christ. One thing became clear, however, to Pugh:

The attack upon our open-air campaign prepared the people of Pontypridd for the great Temperance Movement of January 1882.[3]

---

3 *The Romance of the Forward Movement*, pp. 43–44.

Chapter 5

While pastoring in Tredegar, Pugh had been involved in the Temperance Movement and supported the National Temperance League and the Good Templars, the latter being an international organisation. Pugh established the Templars in Tredegar and was delighted that fifteen hundred locals had joined. Some of the national and American representatives of these related movements were visitors to Pontypridd and spoke in well-attended meetings and missions. An article appeared in the *Pontypridd Chronicle* during 1882 providing a sketch of Pugh's life and work. The journalist—with the pen name, 'Awstin'—describes Pugh's work:

> His constant and consistent opposition to the liquor traffic—for he is the friend of the public and not the publican—brought him into antagonism with the liquor trafficker, and even the magisterial bench which has the power to suppress or advance the greatest enemy of the law. This, on one occasion, almost landed him in Cardiff prison. He was not prepared to apologise to the Bench for the strong things he had uttered about their conduct; but he was quite prepared to go to prison, if that would save the people and open the eyes of the Bench on the evil of strong drink.[4]

Local support was so strong for the evangelist that the Bench had no choice but to drop the case against him.

While the Temperance Movement grew considerably in the area and much to the dismay of the publicans, John Pugh was probably unaware of a young man with a colourful past who had signed the temperance pledge in Pontypridd. The man's name was Seth Joshua. All his friends were shocked that he of all people had taken this radical step. 'A great gospel temperance revival was going on in Gelliwastad Wesleyan Chapel' in 1882, Seth Joshua shared, and 'I signed the pledge'.[5] That in itself was a remarkable step and all his drinking and working friends were amazed at the dramatic change in his life. His conversion took place 'some few weeks afterwards', he records, and almost immediately he began to witness zealously for Christ. However, it was not until about nine years later in

---

4 *The Romance of the Forward Movement*, p. 45.
5 *Seth and Frank Joshua: The Renewed Evangelists*, Rev. T. Mardy Rees (Wrexham, Hughes & Son, Principality Press, 1926), p. 111.

the spring of 1891 at Port Talbot that Seth Joshua met John Pugh, when they walked around the local countryside discussing evangelism. Pugh wanted him to move to Cardiff to engage in evangelism. We will later see that Seth responded and became a real support and encouragement to Pugh in evangelising South Wales and beyond.

Church growth

Pugh's preaching and compassion continued to impact people and significant numbers of people were saved and integrated into the life of the church. A major problem was that their rented hall was too small, so within two years of arriving in Pontypridd a new chapel was built and named as St David's Presbyterian Church. The journalist Awstin described Pugh's preaching as being fiery, carefully prepared, fluent, earnest with his appeals flowing from 'a heart burning with a desire to save souls and a soul imbued with the faith that moves mountains'.[6] This preacher was a man of prayer too, who believed that God blessed the faithful preaching of the gospel. He therefore expected conversions and spiritual growth in converts.

Library

Other details about this ministry in Pontypridd deserve mention here. One detail is the library project for the town. Plans were afoot for a Free Library to be built for the local population, but the public were generally indifferent to the proposal, while those engaged in the sale of alcohol feared a library might attract young people away from their drinking houses. A decision was made to arrange a public vote so that the matter could be settled once and for all. John Pugh was a strong advocate of the Free Library, recognising the need of somewhere else, other than the pubs, for people to go for relaxation. On the day of the vote, the ratepayers cast their votes, but Pugh was concerned they might lose the vote. Near closing time, he knew that several of his church members were away on business and were due to arrive back by train close to the deadline for closing the voting station. There was no time to lose and action was needed.

---

6 *Grace, Grit & Gumption*, p. 32.

Chapter 5

Pugh, with a friend, went to the railway station and met the eight church members off the train and hurried them to the polling station. All eight members of St David's Presbyterian church arrived just in time and voted in favour of the library. When the result was announced the next day, a small majority of eight had secured the establishment of the library!

Concerns

There were other concerns which troubled Pugh, concerns which related to church growth. As the majority of Presbyterian churches at the time held services only in the Welsh language, this meant that the growing numbers of residents and workers in industrial areas unfamiliar with the Welsh language would not be reached with the gospel. Pugh himself, though a fluent Welsh speaker, served as minister of English language churches in Tredegar and Pontypridd for the primary reason of evangelising non-Welsh-speakers. The problem was becoming more acute with Welsh churches hardly addressing the challenge, so that the gulf between chapel and the working class was widening year by year. Pugh was burdened over the issue, yet he needed to act sensitively as nearly all the churches and associations of churches within the Presbyterian church of Wales carried on their work through the medium of Welsh.

In 1884, a small circle of friends met in Pugh's home to discuss the needs and ministry of the English churches. Their decision was to form an English Conference of Presbyterian churches in South Wales. This decision was unofficial, but Pugh was determined to act on the basis of their decision and challenge his denomination. His next step was to invite four other ministers and nine lay people to meet him in St David's Church, Pontypridd on 8th May, 1884 to discuss the issue further. This was a crunch meeting where Pugh shared his concerns for cultural changes like making their public services more relevant, dynamic and geared more to young people unfamiliar with the Christian faith. His friends were in agreement and shared the need for the denomination to recognise the importance of the English language for the sake of gospel communication to the masses of non-Welsh-speakers in South Wales. No time was lost and later in 1884 the first South Wales Conference met at Swansea, and in Pontypridd the

Pontypridd: 1881–1889

following year. The English language churches now had a voice and some influence, with some high-ranking individuals giving their support, like Edward Davies, JP, who served as the first President. He was the son of David Davies, Llandinam, the industrialist, and closer links were made with this family providing excellent support for Pugh's future ministry. By 1889 the chair person of the Conference was Dr T. Charles Edwards who was widely admired and respected within the denomination for his academic achievements, books and preaching. Over the following years, well-known speakers also addressed the Conference like F. B. Meyer (1895), James Denney (1897) the Scottish Presbyterian theologian, P. T. Forsyth (1901), then a year after Pugh's death, Campbell Morgan in 1908.[7] The English Conference achieved its purpose of representing and highlighting the importance as well as the need for English-language churches especially in South Wales. However, the primary motivation of John Pugh throughout this process was not the language but rather the communication of the gospel to English speakers. This was a gospel and not a language issue.

In the next chapter we will retrace some of our steps in order to trace how John Pugh was so well informed concerning evangelism and developments in Christian work in other parts of the United Kingdom as well as in America. That is an important part of the story. Pugh never isolated himself from what was going on further afield. His passion for the gospel and burden to reach those ignorant of the gospel made him open and willing to adopt new methods and approaches if they helped to bring people to hear the gospel. In this respect the names of the Rev. William Ross and the American evangelist Dwight L. Moody are important.

---

7 Sadly, this English Conference, and other sections of the Presbyterian Church of Wales, were influenced by biblical and historical criticism/scepticism from the end of the nineteenth-century. A stalwart like the Rev. William Williams, Swansea, rejected the new methods of biblical criticism in 1894 on the ground that such criticism was refuted by Christ's testimony. But opposition to the traditional view of the Bible was gathering momentum and prestige. In 1900, for example, Professor Ellis Edwards suggested that where necessary the church should revise its position. This suggestion was confirmed by Principal Prys in 1903 who urged the denomination to be unafraid of modifying its view of Scripture and the truths of Scripture. The advice was heeded when a 'Reconstruction Commission' was established in 1919 by the two Welsh language Associations of churches which duly reported 'its unhesitating belief in the right of the church to revise its creed whenever it feels that such a revision is necessary'.

6. Wider contacts and ministry

There is need to step back a little in order to understand some of the major factors leading to Pugh's widening ministry. His fifth year of ministry in Tredegar in 1877 was extremely significant because John Pugh visited Scotland for the first time, a visit which proved to be an important milestone in developing his own evangelism in Wales, while at the same time forging a close relationship with a Scottish minister, the Rev. William Ross (1836–1904). One cannot over-emphasise the importance of this visit for Pugh's consequent ministry. Pugh and Ross became close friends, sharing a mutual passion for evangelism and reaching socially deprived people with the gospel and providing practical help. While Ross became a frequent visitor to South Wales, Pugh also visited Scotland regularly to preach, especially in Glasgow, and was even invited to assist Ross permanently in his work in Glasgow. However, details are sparse concerning his first visit to Rothesay and the factors lying behind Pugh's initial contact with Ross.

The Rev. William Ross had been ordained as a minister of Chapelhill Free Gaelic Church, Rothesay, on the Isle of Bute in 1867, remaining there until 1883. By his third year in Rothesay, church membership stood at 138 and Ross conducted all its services through the medium of Gaelic, the language of the heart which meant a great deal to locals. Immediately prior to his ordination, Ross had written a report on Gaelic education and he would become active in the administration of Gaelic schools in the Highlands. As John Pugh was himself fluent in Welsh and English, this may have been a significant factor in drawing the two men closer together, especially as Ross had a growing concern for Gaelic speakers who were becoming more mobile in their search for work in Scotland.

Wider contacts and ministry

Dwight L. Moody

Another important detail is that during the summer of 1874 the American evangelist, Dwight L. Moody (1837–1899) preached at meetings in many parts of Scotland. In Aberdeen, nearly 24,000 crowded into an amphitheatre to listen to the gospel; then he spoke in Montrose, Brechin, Huntley (where 15,000 listened to him in the open air), Inverness, Arbroath, Tain, Nairn, and Elgin, and other places visited included Rothesay.

Moody's first of several visits to Britain had been in 1867 with his wife, the year of Ross's ordination, when the American evangelist met many Christians from various parts of England and had been thrilled to meet Charles Spurgeon and visit George Müller in Bristol to see the incredible work being done in caring for many orphans without any public appeals for money. His visit and the startling news of the crowds flocking to hear him preach in London and beyond were relayed to the public by newspapers and Christian magazines. There was an air of excitement among Christians all over the country.

Other visits followed, some in quick succession, but for our interest Ross would have met and listened to Moody on his visit to Rothesay in 1874 and he may well have travelled to other areas in Scotland to hear the evangelist beforehand. Moody's extended mission in Edinburgh from late November 1873 has been described as an 'Awakening' because of its impact on churches and unchurched people. The mission attracted considerable attention in Scotland with many invitations being extended to the evangelist to visit their area. Consequently, many other towns, cities and villages in subsequent months were included in his itinerary, including Rothesay.

Three aspects of Moody's influence are relevant at this point. One aspect was his passion to communicate the gospel message to people both in and outside of the churches. In one address given during his visit to Sheffield in 1874, for example, he asked a searching and pertinent question:

What is to be done for the unsaved masses?

He then explained that he had found 'a spiritual famine in England' he had never imagined existed:

Chapter 6

Here, for instance, in this town of Sheffield, I am told that there are one hundred and fifty thousand people who not only never go near a place of worship, but for whom there is actually no church accommodation provided, even if they were willing to take advantage of it. It seems to me that if there be upon God's earth one blacker sight than these thousands of Christless and graceless souls, it is the thousands of dead and slumbering Christians living in their very midst, rubbing shoulders with them every day upon the streets, and never so much as lifting up a little finger to warn them of death and eternity and judgment to come. Talk of being sickened at the sight of the world's degradation, ah! let those of us who are Christians hide our faces because of our own, and pray God to deliver us from the guilt of the world's blood. I believe that if there is one thing which pierces the Master's heart with unutterable grief, it is not the world's iniquity, but the church's indifference.[1]

He then argued that it was the responsibility of all Christians, not only the minister and church officers, to reach out to the masses of people outside the church. This became a growing conviction for Ross and it was a burden that John Pugh shared deeply, and so he must have been delighted to hear of the ways in which Moody reached out to unchurched unbelievers who were ignorant of the gospel.

Another aspect of Moody's influence was the new approach he adopted in evangelism. Modifying the traditionalist and formal approach of church services, he introduced new contemporary songs suitable for evangelistic meetings, and Ira Sankey was influential in this respect. Moody's preaching was direct, basic, interesting and biblical, with ample illustrations in which he expected spiritual responses from his hearers concerning faith in Christ and a willingness to serve Christ fully. His 'appeal' to hearers to indicate publicly by standing, then being counselled afterwards if they wanted to become Christians or dedicate their lives to Christ, met with a huge response, although questioned by some critics. What is certain, nevertheless, is that he held the attention of congregations, whether in

---

[1] *The Life of Dwight L. Moody*, by his son William R. Moody, Official Authorised Edition (1900 version), p. 184.

Wider contacts and ministry

churches or outside, and that many responses by individuals were genuine, resulting in changed and sanctified lives.

New hymns and Christian songs were introduced by Moody in his meetings, many of which were authored by Ira Sankey who was a popular singer in the mission meetings. While in Rothesay, Ross was opposed to singing hymns in public worship, favouring exclusive psalmody, but he changed his view after moving to Glasgow when faced with so many unchurched people in the area. Moody and Sankey visited Glasgow for missions and Ross soon deemed it appropriate to adopt modern hymns and songs, which he did so with enthusiasm, using a minimum of four different hymn books for his congregation regularly! As we have seen, Pugh was much more open and in touch with the new songs being written, which is illustrated in his use of the new hymn, 'I hear Thy welcome voice' in Tredegar within months of its being published.

Pugh was similar to Ross in terms of personality and warmth. Both men were relational, loving people, engaging in friendship with different types of individuals and backgrounds but deeply concerned over the socially needy folk who were often in deep poverty, suffering in countless ways as a result of alcohol abuse and infidelity. More importantly, both men had an intense love for Christ and a burden to share the gospel of Christ with unbelievers. The love of Christ constrained them in all aspects of their work whether preaching, pastoring or providing for the practical needs of the socially deprived. Here were men passionate in their love of Christ, with a longing for as many people as possible to come to know and trust in the Saviour of sinners.

It is no surprise therefore that Pugh visited Scotland almost annually to preach in missions after Ross moved to Glasgow in 1883, and was greatly loved by the people for his ministry and support. Ross too was a frequent visitor to Wales, encouraging Pugh and others in their evangelism in industrial areas. The type of work undertaken by Pugh in the Forward Movement was inspired by what he witnessed in Ross's parish church in Cawcaddens, Glasgow. No wonder that Ross was honoured by being invited to speak several times on the occasion of the General Assembly meetings of the Presbyterian Church of Wales in 1899.

Chapter 6

Influence

The influence of Ross in this continuing friendship was considerable and confirmatory in several ways. For example, it served to confirm Pugh's deep concern that churches were too respectable and detached from the working classes, and Ross agreed, for a similar situation prevailed in Scotland. Again, while both Ross and Pugh loved their first languages, Gaelic and Welsh, they recognised the pressing need to evangelise those who understood only English. Possibly Pugh identified the need first as Ross was heavily committed to Gaelic speakers and the development of Gaelic education from the time he was in Rothesay. Both men, too, with their passionate love of Christ, longed to declare Christ's gospel to unbelievers, especially the unchurched and socially needy. For Ross this was the primary aim of his ministry, despite the extensive humanitarian work initiated through his church. This conviction was shared by Pugh. Their friendship therefore was confirmatory in many ways, providing mutual encouragement, direction, fellowship and prayer through their regular visits to each other's areas of work. Pugh was always warmly welcomed to Glasgow where his preaching and support for their minister was valued.

Pugh's evangelism in South Wales developed in slightly different ways from that in Cowcaddens. Ross worked out his local church principle consistently. Beginning his ministry in Cowcaddens with only one hundred members, he immediately undertook to prepare and mobilise all the members to participate in evangelism, while those gifted to lead in varied aspects of outreach and practical help received training and supervision. The church building was open each evening and regular open-air meetings arranged. This was not a one-man mission entirely dependent on the minister but rather engagement by the entire church. Within five years, the church membership had increased to 1,249 and mostly by conversions, with the Sunday School having 1,192 in attendance and a strong Bible Class of men totalling 470. The extent of this work was remarkable and before long there were two assistant ministers with two men and four women serving as missionaries in the parish. A Pioneer Mission was formed within the church to serve women in the area, which involved teams usually of two young women living in the heart of the slums area who visited, nursed, advised and encouraged as many women as they could.

The growth was startling but clearly achieved by means of prayer, preaching, training, fellowship and corporate involvement by members. By contrast, Pugh was disappointed by the lack of support on the part of his church officers and members when he first engaged in open-air preaching in his three pastorates. Too often he was alone, although in Tredegar four elderly women from the church arrived to stand alongside him on the first occasion. In Pontypridd he was alone in the first open-air meetings in a notoriously dangerous area of the town and relied on a rough character who volunteered to provide Pugh with protection from the hostile crowd gathered around.

A further difference, as we will see, is that Ross majored in evangelising his parish and immediate area, whereas Pugh reached out to various industrial areas in South Wales, especially where the people were ignorant of the gospel. The whole of Wales was also within his vision. Open-air preaching was conducted in different areas with the use of a tent, and then, if the response was encouraging, a temporary wooden hut was built for meetings prior to providing a large hall. Following several visits to Cowcaddens, the idea of a Forward Movement engaged in evangelism and church planting over a wider area was conceived in Pugh's mind, but its implementation was gradual. Ross's encouragement for Pugh in this developing work was invaluable.

In continuing the story of John Pugh, we will observe how he and Ross benefited from mutual support and fellowship in what was a pioneer work both in Glasgow and in Wales. On one of Ross's many visits to Wales, he preached at the third Anniversary of the Memorial Hall Centre on Sunday 17th June, 1894, and then the following evening gave a 'powerful address on "Aggressive Christianity"'.[2]

---

2 *The Monthly Treasury*, Vol. 1, No. 7, July 1894, p. 17.

7. Cardiff: an epicentre

The year is 1888, and the location is Pontypridd where Pugh had been a Presbyterian church minister for eight years. The church had grown considerably due to his zeal in sharing the gospel with unchurched people and consequently the church growth experienced was due mostly to the influx of many converts. Early in his ministry it had been necessary to build a new and more spacious chapel, near the town centre, called St David's Presbyterian Church. Other converts settled into churches nearer their homes, but the good news of Jesus Christ crucified for the salvation of sinners, risen victoriously from the dead, had been preached faithfully throughout the town and area without fear or compromise. The Temperance Movement also witnessed an unusual degree of growth as converts and others saw the distressing consequences of alcohol abuse and abandoned their previous habits. Pugh had worked tirelessly in the town.

Towards the end of the year, Pugh received invitations to pastor in two different churches. One invitation was to become assistant minister to his friend, the Rev. William Ross in Cowcaddens, Glasgow. This was an attractive invitation and 'he was sorely tempted to migrate to Glasgow, in order to be near his great friend'.[1] Pugh's daughter described Ross as her father's 'bosom friend'.[2] The appeal of this invitation, therefore, needs to be appreciated, for he would be sharing ministry with a man he admired and was close to. Was it a foregone conclusion he would go to Scotland?

The second invitation was to a church in nearby Cardiff. Pugh's daughter draws attention to her father's sense of being drawn providentially to the Cardiff rather than the Glasgow church. Church members and other friends did not want Pugh to leave Pontypridd and put pressure on him to remain as their minister, but Pugh 'felt that the call from Cardiff had

---

1 *The Romance of the Forward Movement*, pp. 47–48.
2 *Atgofion am John Pugh*, pp. 16–17.

Cardiff: an epicentre

come from God'. One pressing factor in the decision was that St David's Church in Pontypridd which he had served was 'way ahead of the Cardiff church in numbers and spirituality'. His awareness, too, of the appalling spiritual and practical needs of people in South Wales and his love for the Presbyterian Church of Wales all contributed in confirming the call to Cardiff rather than to Glasgow. Pugh also knew that the Cardiff church was located in a densely populated area and that more and more people were moving into the area looking for work. The church concerned was Clifton Street Presbyterian Church, Newport Road, close to the town centre. This was a young church planted in 1868 by a Welsh language church in the Docks area. A few years before Pugh started there, the Clifton Street church decided to become an English language church, thereby adapting to the changing character of the growing population while retaining its traditional approach to church worship and practice. January 1889, therefore, marked a new chapter for the church when its new minister, the Rev. John Pugh, was inducted. Could this church and Cardiff itself become an epicentre of a powerful movement by the Lord in saving many people and reviving believers? Pugh had a growing conviction that Cardiff was a key location for a wider ministry to unbelievers. And he was not mistaken either.

First things first

The first Sunday Pugh preached in his Cardiff church set the tone for the future direction of the work. Church members knew that God had spoken to them that day and Pugh was surprised at the freedom and authority he experienced in preaching. The Lord was at work. Members were subdued following the evening service, so Pugh invited them to join him for a time of prayer. His daughter recalls the evening:

That unforgettable prayer meeting, the thing was so new, so striking, so strange! It all comes back so vividly—the old-fashioned school room beneath the chapel, the solemn minister; no noisy excitement, only a quiet gravity which couldn't be described coming over the people. Then, as the meeting went on, first one and then another going forward until twenty-two souls knelt in repentance before God.

Chapter 7

One of the church officers was delighted, expressing how for years there had been a lack of God's power evident in their worship services.

The opening week in January in his new pastorate was devoted to church prayer meetings each evening. Although a regular custom in churches at the start of a new year, for Pugh it was essential to have the people praying and seeking the Lord's blessing upon the work. Lying behind his emphasis on prayer was his conviction that only the Lord could change the situation and grow the church with conversions. Prayer should be central both personally and corporately.

One senses his excitement in settling into his new sphere of labour with its enormous challenges. And he lost no time in getting to work. Following the week of prayer, he arranged a two-week mission and Pugh was delighted when other pastors in the area supported this outreach. 'The mission was a tremendous success, resulting in many hundreds being added to the churches of the Roath district.'[3] Rather than two weeks, the mission continued unbroken for three months with daily prayer meetings at 7.00 am, Bible readings at 3.00 pm and evangelistic services at 7–7.30 pm. This mission later led to the re-emergence of 'The Roath United Mission'.[4]

There were other changes taking place in his own church, too. One Sunday each month Dr Cynddylan Jones (1840–1930) preached in Clifton Street. He had pastored churches in Pontypool and London and at this time pastored an English language church in Frederick Street, Cardiff. He was a well known and popular preacher both in Welsh and in English and authored several books expounding the Scriptures. While it was a privilege to have Dr Cynddylan Jones preach in the church once a month, Pugh noticed that the congregation was not large and those attending tended to be middle-class. His daughter relates how her father urged the famous preacher to minister the Word to believers while at the same time he himself would 'go after the sinners' outside. That is what happened!

---

3 *The Romance of the Forward Movement*, p. 49.
4 This was given a new name by Pugh who widened its scope and basis under the name of 'The Cardiff United Mission'.

Cardiff: an epicentre

Burden

Pugh's vision and burden extended beyond the church and the immediate locality. Significantly, for a two-year period he studied closely the building developments in Cardiff, housing plans and other developments which involved him in interviewing those in local authorities regarding their schemes, and he visited sites where building was in progress. One of his motives was to identify suitable sites for a church building, then to purchase the sites before they were used for other purposes. His church members were not as enthusiastic as they ought to have been. For example, he saw the immediate opportunity of evangelising the nearby but distinctive area of Splott and shared the needs of that area with his church members. They were not opposed to his plan to evangelise there but they failed to give him the enthusiastic encouragement and support he desired. Being a man of action, and burdened for people to be saved, he obtained a favourable site for a church tent, then eventually a building would be erected.

Cardiff prison

Within months[5] of settling in Cardiff, Pugh was walking nearby to the prison when he observed small groups of men standing near the prison and clearly waiting for something to happen or someone to appear. He realised quickly they were expecting their friends or partners in crime to be released from prison. Pugh decided to stop and watch what went on. At several intervals, a man walked out of prison and his group warmly welcomed him and led him away. This happened several times. Pugh was saddened to realise that the motive of these groups was to employ some of the released prisoners to assist them in committing further crimes in the future. He was troubled. What could be done? Where were the Christians to help? He decided he had to do something about the situation. The first thing he did was to write to the newspaper, inviting friends to get involved in helping those being released from prison. He then wrote to two men of influence and wealth, the Cory brothers who were involved

---

5   June 1890.

Chapter 7

in a shipping and coal business. Would they be willing to help? Both John and Richard Cory responded positively and became president and treasurer respectively. The three men arranged to meet the governor of the prison to share their plans and to seek his support. Formal support was given and quickly a few volunteers were chosen to stand outside the prison daily at 8.00 am with an invitation to each released prisoner, man or woman, to a free breakfast where hymns would be sung and a gospel message given. Within one year, more than two thousand ex-prisoners had responded to the invitation to the breakfast, with some of them being converted, and so the Society for the Aid of Released Prisoners had been launched successfully.

American visitors

The visit to Cardiff of the American evangelist Dwight L. Moody and his musical companion Ira D. Sankey left a deep impression on Pugh. The Americans conducted a mission during 1891 in the former Wood Street Congregational Church in the town centre which at the time was the largest church building in Cardiff and seated about two thousand people. Pugh was encouraged but surprised by the large numbers of people who crowded into the meetings. Daily, and from early morning, there would be a long queue of people eager to enter the church for a meeting. Pugh took his daughter Annie along to hear Moody as he was eager for her to have the experience and also have assurance concerning her faith in Christ. His own conviction strengthened even more during this mission, namely that churches were failing in their commission to reach the multitudes with the gospel. Quoting Tennyson, he felt that churches had killed their Christ.[6] Pugh also took his daughter with him to visit Moody who was staying in the home of Richard Cory. Moody was impressed with Pugh's passion and work for the gospel and wanted him to return to Chicago with him. The response of Pugh was immediate. For Pugh, Cardiff was 'the Chicago of Wales'! He was called to work in the area and his daughter described his response:

---

6 *Atgofion am John Pugh*, pp. 20–21.

Cardiff: an epicentre

It is estimated that the number of seats in Cardiff's churches, chapels ... is 54,000, and having allowed the most generous estimate for regular churchgoers, the serious fact faces us that around two thirds of the inhabitants of Cardiff are complete strangers to the House of God ... the influence for good displayed by different dominations is great, but so insignificant in terms of dealing with the increasing evil of this large town! When we think of the general apathy towards the means of grace; the disgraceful forms of drunkenness and pollution; the steady and persistent movement led by the Free-Thinkers, those who claim the name Christians, to profane the Lord's Day; and the craving for pleasures and frivolity, the great number of 'lower class' which are in our midst with their condition calling for improvement, I must stay in Cardiff.

Within two years, his own church in Clifton Street had become numerically and spiritually strong, but the majority of people outside the churches troubled and burdened him more and more. Where should he start in developing a wider work?

Splott

John Pugh was concerned to reach as many unsaved people as possible. Despite his busy life, he spent much time in private and prayed with others too when this was possible for this outreach. Planning was also involved. For example, he familiarised himself with the areas in closer proximity to Clifton Street, discovering where the new houses were being built. He was also in touch with influential business people like the Cory brothers. The gospel of Christ was precious to him and the unchurched people needed to hear this good news. Their needs were desperate. Once again he shared the needs with his church, especially the area of Splott which was within walking distance of their church. No enthusiastic support was forthcoming from church members or officers although they did not oppose his plan. Once again he appeared to be on his own. One discouraging comment made was that Pugh's attempts to convert the people of Splott and using a tent for meetings in the first place was like trying to demolish the Fort of Gibraltar with boiled peas! In his typical response, Pugh emphasised that the gospel was God's dynamite which was 'capable of blowing up

Chapter 7

the firmest of Satan's strongholds'.[7] His faith was strong and his resolve to preach to people in Splott was not weakened by the scepticism of church people.

William Ross's work in Glasgow in reaching the unchurched with the gospel continued to encourage Pugh. After all, Splott was densely populated with working men with little spiritual provision for them. Providentially, he obtained a suitable site in which to erect a tent for evangelistic meetings. He was poised for action. However, there were at least three major factors to consider.

Major factors

First of all, he was the minister of a growing church in Clifton Street and preached there most Sundays. He did not shirk his pulpit or pastoral responsibilities despite his zeal for evangelism. However, if his workload increased with a new work in Splott, how would he cope?

A second factor to consider was that of support both in terms of prayer and of finance. While Ross in Glasgow had the full and enthusiastic support of his entire church, that was not true of Pugh. Clifton Street admired their minister, valued his preaching and care, but did not share the vision and burden he had for the unsaved in the area. This was a problem compounded by Pugh's growing desire and concern to reach the whole of Cardiff and the industrial areas beyond with the gospel and provide humanitarian relief. Here was one of the ways in which Ross and Pugh differed in their approach. Ross was parish based and worked from within the local church by training and equipping the membership for their involvement in the work. For Ross, it was 'better to plough a small field than scratch a whole acre', and in that work the local congregation of believers was heavily involved. By contrast, Pugh lacked active, enthusiastic support from his own congregation while his vision extended to new areas for pioneer evangelism. Who would support and accompany him in this work?

---

7 *The Romance of the Forward Movement*, p. 60.

Cardiff: an epicentre

The third factor was a crucial one: where would he find the workers to assist and even relieve him in this growing work? It was clearly too much for one person to handle. Were there people willing to assume responsibilities for this new work? He needed men and women who loved Christ, His gospel and sinners, no matter who they were and how far they had sunk in sin. In Pugh's own words, he needed helpers who had 'grit, grace and gumption'. Their work would be extremely difficult and demanding as well as exhausting. Such workers needed hearts filled with the love and grace of the Lord Jesus Christ. They needed grit and courage to face dangerous situations and the threats of those who opposed the work. Gumption and wisdom were essential too. Were there such people available? Aware of the Lord's words that 'the harvest truly is plentiful, but the labourers are few', Pugh prayed often as the Lord had commanded: 'Therefore pray the Lord of the harvest to send out labourers into His harvest' (Matthew 9:37–38).

During the months of 1891, Pugh began to think of a man who could be suitable for the work. His name was Seth Joshua who was being used effectively with his brother in the town of Neath. Pugh needed to meet him and seek his help. That is the story of the next chapter.

8. More gospel action and Seth Joshua

The location is the Welsh Baptist Chapel in Upper Trosant in Pontypool. Seth Joshua was one of six children whose parents and grandmother were members of the chapel. His grandmother, 'Granny Walden', cleaned and looked after the chapel building. The pastor was the Rev. David Roberts who was a powerful preacher of God's Word. Granny Walden was a Christian who was strong in her love for the Lord and His Word. She taught her six grandchildren Bible verses regularly and her prayers for them were answered eventually in conversions and with three grandsons becoming pastors, namely, Caleb, Frank and Seth. As a caretaker of the Welsh chapel, she often enjoyed the opportunity of discussing Bible sermons and doctrines with preachers. She was a character, a strict disciplinarian, but Seth was a problem to her as a child for he was mischievous and rebellious. Granny Walden was concerned for him and warned that his behaviour could end in disaster. That fact frightened Seth.

David Roberts, the pastor, was a gifted preacher who influenced Seth and his peers; his brother Caleb later became a Baptist pastor. Seth too was quietly impressed by the pastor's preaching, even imagining himself becoming a preacher one day. One weekday morning, Seth went into their Baptist church pulpit unnoticed and pretended to preach like the pastor while thumping the Bible occasionally as he did so. On this occasion, his grandmother walked in and, assuming he was mocking the preacher, threatened to punish him. As he ran away the old lady threw her broom at him which just missed its target!

Unlike his peers, Seth often played truant from school but later regretted it. His first job was driving a donkey and he did this for nearly four years. He found this job helpful and instructive:

More gospel action and Seth Joshua

I had more out of that donkey than I could get out of any College in the land. If I put his head one way he would put it the other; so I used to put his tail always toward the direction I wanted him to go. I bear many marks of his back-kicks on my lower extremities. He was a great donkey to object. I maintain that if a man knows how to handle a donkey ... he is qualified to handle anything awkward.[1]

Seth then worked for the railway, played rugby for Pontypool where he excelled, but slowly gambling and alcohol took a grip on his life. His family moved from Pontypool to Treforest near Pontypridd where Seth and his father obtained work at the local iron works. Life was exciting as Seth became the life and soul of parties in the local tavern where he sang and entertained folk. When the Salvation Army advertised their mission to the town he planned to disturb their meetings. However, observing the Salvation Army with their instruments and hearing their prayer and message, Seth was subdued; but he was more shocked the next day to hear that Frank had been converted and had joined them. Invited to a gospel temperance meeting in a Wesleyan church where an American speaker appealed for people to abandon alcohol, Seth went forward and became an abstainer, to the surprise of those present. In a further meeting, he was converted.

Providence

Ten years after their conversion, an unexpected providence in 1882 found brothers Frank and Seth living together in the town of Neath. Their close relationship and their shared love for the Lord led them immediately to launch what became a fruitful period of evangelism and church planting in the town. Their aim was to declare Christ to as many people as possible, wherever and whoever they were. Frank had arrived in time to speak and sing to the crowds attending the famous annual September Fair which continued for a week. Many miners from the valleys and local tin workers flocked into town to enjoy themselves. Beer drinking, excess, fighting and indecent behaviour were prominent in the Fair, so that many of the local people never ventured out during the evenings.

---
1 *Seth and Frank Joshua*, p. 5.

Chapter 8

However, for Seth and Frank the opportunity to witness was God-given and they feared no one but God. Witnessing in the Fair became an annual event for them. Neither had received training in preaching or evangelism, but when Seth arrived they immediately began to use rooms in local churches for meetings and maintain open-air preaching. Then they were given a tent to use which attracted crowds of people, even when it was leaking due to heavy rain. Seth was honest in describing their witness:

Neither of us could preach a sermon. I know now what a sermon is, but I did not know then any more than the man in the moon. Frank would sing, and I would pray, and then we would sing a duet, and then we would give our testimonies. Although we had no preparation, praise God, hundreds were saved.[2]

The impact of these meetings and the number of regular conversions had an impact on the town and area, while meetings were held in churches by the brothers for prayer, fellowship and preaching. The local rector, an evangelical who was also Archdeacon of Llandaff, supported the Joshua brothers and the converts, often giving them communion early on Sunday mornings. The increasing numbers of people attending their meetings meant that the local church buildings became too small and so the foundation stone for the first Mission Hall was laid in April 1884 with accommodation intended for one thousand people. Frank and Seth did not receive a salary while in Neath. Unlike his brother, Seth was married and was the means of bringing his wife, Mary, to the Lord. Her own testimony illustrates their poverty but also their strong faith in the Lord:

When I look back I am filled with wonder and praise. It was a most amazing time, living by faith and yet wanting nothing. I never handled a salary till we went to Cardiff. Whenever I wanted anything, Seth would say 'Pray first, Mary, and when you receive never forget to return thanks.' His faith was endless.[3]

---

2 *Seth and Frank Joshua*, p. 15.
3 *Seth and Frank Joshua*, p. 18.

Progress in Neath

Open-air preaching which included singing and testimonies was a dominant feature of the evangelism undertaken by the brothers. While they faced constant opposition and interruptions, they continued to reach hundreds of people who had no links with churches. Their biographer who witnessed events during this period claims that in the open air 'they found scores of their most remarkable converts'.[4] People were converted in various locations in the town and vicinity; when they were under conviction of sin and could bear the pressure no longer, they knelt and trusted Christ. Often outside a public house, a lodging house, in the cattle market, the square, on a grass verge or in a street, individuals made their peace with God, unashamed even if people observed them praying to God for mercy. While he was singing a hymn, Seth relates how one man came near to him, knelt and 'gave himself to the Lord'. Sunday services too were blessed with a prayer meeting at 7.30 am, an open-air before the 11.00 am preaching service, then Sunday School in the afternoon and another open-air preceding the evening preaching service at the Mission Hall which had been specially built for the growing work.

Prayer was central in what was happening. Some evenings as many as five cottage prayer meetings were held by the converts and there are frequent references to 'good prayer meetings'. Both Seth and brother Frank gave themselves to prayer in their busy schedule and observed family worship. In his diary, the following entries describe their ongoing concern in prayer for the Lord's divine help:

Monday, 14 Feb, 1887. We spent a precious time in prayer at two o'clock today. We are praying for a general revival of religion in Neath.

Sat, 2 Feb, 1889. We all agreed to lay hold of God for the blessing upon Neath. My soul is much exercised. I could not eat my dinner today on account of it.

---

4 *Seth and Frank Joshua*, p. 20.

Chapter 8

Friday, 15 Feb, 1889. There is a growing desire to see God's work revive. I feel sure God is not going to leave us much longer without His Divine blessing upon Neath.

6 Aug, 1889. The deadness of things weighed me down. I was not better until I swept away the heaviness and had much prayer.[5]

At the end of 1889, Seth wrote that 'God had permitted me this year to see 455 souls seeking Christ', and the previous year the total was estimated at being 348.

In the spring of 1891, the partnership of Seth and Frank in gospel work in Neath ended with Frank assuming full responsibility for the flourishing church at Neath where he was faithfully supported by believers.[6] The ending of the partnership was wise and Seth describes what happened:

One day I said to Frank, dear old mam and dad are old, and I feel I must leave you. The church is growing strong here now, so you get mam and dad to Neath and make a home for them, and I will go away and take the tent up to the Rhondda Valley. This is all I did, but a boy who will do that for his mam and dad will never be forgotten. I don't want any praise, I simply cleared off.[7]

Wider work

John Pugh had heard a great deal about the work being undertaken by the Joshua brothers in Neath. In the spring of 1891, as Pugh was praying and searching for workers to join him in Cardiff, he thought of Seth and then arranged to have afternoon tea with him in the home of a local pastor in Port Talbot. Afterwards they walked the countryside nearby and shared their concern. Pugh wanted him to work in Cardiff and abandon his plan to go to the Rhondda with his tent. Seth needed a few days to consider the

---

5 *Seth and Frank Joshua*, p. 29.
6 The work prospered and in 1901 the Free Mission Church, Neath with 350 members was constituted as a branch of the Forward Movement of the Presbyterian Church of Wales and Frank was formally ordained by the Welsh Calvinistic Methodist Association as their minister.
7 *Seth and Frank Joshua*, pp. 56–57.

More gospel action and Seth Joshua

request. It was probably during those following days that he visited Pugh in Cardiff who takes up the story:

One day, who should turn up at my house but Mr Seth Joshua. During our conversation he said that some longing had taken possession of his heart to co-operate with me in my efforts to evangelise Cardiff. I clearly saw at once that God had sent him to me, and soon told him all that was on my heart ... I had realised for some time that the Mission conducted by the Joshua brothers in Neath could very well spare one of them. So, after my first interview with Seth Joshua, I encouraged him to join me in Cardiff. I could not, however, pledge myself that his salary would be always certain, for at that time there was no church or committee or fund at my back. If we had waited for a big fund to be collected, we would never have started the Forward Movement in Cardiff.[8]

Prayer was being answered and Seth accepted the invitation immediately and left Neath for Cardiff with his wife and six children. He and his wife believed the Lord would supply all their needs. Seth took his borrowed tent with him to Cardiff which he intended to use for evangelism in the East Moors area of Splott.

The story is worth repeating for the occasion was significant, marking the opening of a new and brave venture in reaching the unchurched working class in the area. In fact, the story involving the partnership of Seth Joshua and John Pugh led later to the formation of the Forward Movement within the Presbyterian church of Wales. The story is factual, too.

On a Saturday morning in May 1891 in the area of East Moors in the Splott area of Cardiff, two men started erecting a large tent on a vacant piece of land close to industry, the docks and homes which were being built for the growing population. Seth Joshua was the younger man and experienced in erecting tents, whereas John Pugh, now middle-aged and suffering from lumbago, was inexperienced with regard to erecting tents. It was Seth who used the heavy sledgehammer to place the pegs firmly in place to secure the tent safely into the ground, while Pugh was the assistant. At last the tent appeared secure and impressive, almost ready

---

8 *The Romance of the Forward Movement*, pp. 60–61.

Chapter 8

for use, when a local labourer enquired what was happening: 'Is this a boxing show?' he asked. Seth was quick in responding: 'There is going to be some fighting here.' The man then wanted to know the time and who the opponents were? Seth informed him that the fighting would take place the next morning on the Sunday at 11.00 am and the opponent was a 'chap called Beelzebub'. The labourer had never heard the name and so was informed: 'He's a smart one, I can tell you. Come tomorrow morning.' And the man turned up for the service in the tent as promised and during the first hymn realised what was happening. And he was converted in that service and became one of the first converts in this outreach to East Moors but with many more people to follow in finding new life and forgiveness in Christ. For a week before the tent was opened, the young people in Pugh's church in Clifton Street visited the houses in Splott, distributing invitations to the tent services. Their reception was not always favourable, with Pugh's own daughter receiving an angry response from one lady who spat in her face—but she too was converted in the tent soon afterwards.

Workers

The burden of the preaching on Sunday mornings and evenings in the tent fell to Seth for the first few weeks as Pugh was preaching in his own church. But each Sunday afternoon he preached in the tent. Crowds of people attended these services and this heartening response led Pugh after four weeks to erect another tent in nearby Canton, an area thickly populated with dockers and factory workers. The critical question concerned the provision of preachers/evangelists to work with Pugh among the unchurched working class. Seth Joshua would pioneer the work in Canton—but was Pugh opening centres too quickly and without gifted preachers immediately available to him? He lacked an enthusiastic home church with gifted men trained with preaching and evangelistic gifts for such areas. On the other hand, Pugh's deep concern to reach the unchurched in industrial areas gave him a sense of urgency, with the result that he felt restless and 'crushed in spirit' for those who had not heard of Christ. He also knew that many of the men training for the ministry of the

More gospel action and Seth Joshua

Presbyterian Church of Wales were unsuited for this type of evangelism and pastoral work.

In the Lord's providence, Howell G. Howell came to Pugh's attention. He had been brought up in Skewen, Neath, and after his conversion at the age of nineteen he began to help the Joshua brothers in their Mission in Neath. His concern to share the gospel with unbelievers resulted in a strong sense of call to do the work of an evangelist, itinerating, preaching the gospel, holding missions in London, in North Wales, and in towns in the Lancashire, Shropshire and Northampton areas, and he saw many people converted. Returning to South Wales in 1888, he was aware of the need for evangelists within the Presbyterian Church of Wales. He received invitations to hold short and longer missions 'which have been marvellously blessed of the Lord...'.[9]

Some reports of his preaching are encouraging to read. For example, the Rev. W. Evans, Pembroke Dock, reports on a series of evangelistic services Howell conducted in November 1890 and January 1891 for several days at a time and then for a week:

There was a deep yearning in the church for the ingathering of souls ... services were greatly blessed. The divine power was manifest and powerfully felt. In two visits, 70 people were added to the Lord; there was no unhealthy excitement in the meetings but all the people were moved and intense earnestness prevailed ... Mr Howell has 'the precious gift ... for reaping'. If the churches are thus to be blessed they must labour faithfully in sowing the seed and pray earnestly for the divine blessing and longingly await the manifestation of Divine power in the saving of souls ... Mr Howell is well qualified to do the work of an evangelist.

Mr J. Lewis, on behalf of the Rev. Powell in Pembroke, also wrote:

Special evangelistic services were held ... in November 1890, when a series of impressive and successful discourses were delivered by Mr H. G. Howell. The whole of the week preceding the mission was devoted to special prayer by the church ...

---
9 *The Christian Standard*, No. 7, 1892, p. 2.

Chapter 8

thirty were then added to the church ... Mr Howell ... is eminently qualified for evangelistic work ...'.

Pugh's invitation to this man to lead the work in East Moors, Splott, therefore, was a wise one and Mr Howell began there in July 1891:

> I found in him a veritable Stonewall Jackson, who stuck to his post morning and night, and who never gave up a position once he had his foot down.[10]

Howell was the type of evangelist Pugh was praying for to join him in taking the gospel to the multitudes of unchurched people in the industrial areas of Wales.

Appeal

While Pugh was opening the work in East Moors in May 1891 under Seth Joshua, he also inaugurated the Cardiff Evangelical Movement. Some months later he wrote a front page article in their monthly magazine, *The Christian Standard*,[11] entitled 'An Earnest Appeal' in which he requested 'immediate and generous help' from readers and churches. In doing so, he provided a helpful sketch of what had been happening. He had felt for some time that new ways must 'be adopted' if thousands of perishing souls in Cardiff were to be reached and rescued:

> So, after much prayer, and corresponding with friends far and near, we plunged into the breach and through the cooperation of good men and Seth Joshua of Neath Mission, we inaugurated our Plan of Campaign in May 1891 by pitching our first tent on East Moors.

Why East Moors and why their chosen site? East Moors for Pugh was 'the most needy spot in Cardiff with its drink abuse, low morals and violence'. He also refers to Wesleyan, Baptist and Anglican Halls located

---

10 *The Romance of the Forward Movement*, p. 66.
11 Volume 1, Nos. 8 & 9, February & March 1892; 13; pp. 1–2.

More gospel action and Seth Joshua

in the 'most respectable streets away from the worst part of the Moors' and continued:

But we felt led of God to pitch our Tent on the most heathenish spot … we began with mixed feelings of faith and fear but … our fears were soon dispelled … now persuaded that Satan was largely at the bottom of all our doubts and fears for God gave us great favour with the people. Instead of having our tent torn to pieces as prophesied by 'little faith', the poor people thronged to hear the Word of Life preached and sung. Our Senior Evangelist (Seth Joshua) was the pioneer of the campaign on East Moors. Through his earnest, soul-stirring preaching and singing he won his way at once into the hearts of the people. The power of God so rested upon His young servant, that his words burned into the hearts and consciences of his hearers and the large tent became full of the glory of the Lord, like the tent in the wilderness. The people felt God was indeed in the place. The result was that very many gave up their evil ways, rejoicing to the better land. The tent was crowded, folk waded through water and mud to the tent even when rain and winds threatened to blow the canvas away! The work so prospered that we purchased a smaller tent for children … hundreds of children were most anxious to join us … This again turned out to be of God and a great and a good work was begun among the children … The secret of all this … is that the children discovered that workers loved them. Love is the great key. No one can be successful in God's work and soul-saving unless they possess a passionate love for God and souls. This is our experience. O for more and more love for Jesus and people!

The extension of the work to children posed further challenges for Pugh, especially the need for more workers and resources. But in the article, the writer continued the story of East Moors:

Then East Moors Centre had to part with Seth Joshua for he was called to open a new mission centre at Riverside, Canton. Who would succeed him? My thoughts were directed to H. G. Howell who was doing the work of an evangelist … all over the country. So we wrote to him and got a favourable reply … Nothing but faith in God could have induced him to undertake such a tremendous task. And the Lord has rewarded his faith and his labour of love, by giving him marvellous favour with the people and many souls … The Lord put His seal upon this choice at once and

Chapter 8

continues to do so. The people ... love him with a passionate love ... and he brought joy to their hearts and homes. He has a most devoted band of helpers ... in his in-door and out-door work.

Fierce gales and torrential rain destroyed the tent in East Moors and a decision was made not to use tents any more. A temporary wooden building was constructed quickly, seating 500, and this was full on Sundays. 'The number of the saved go on increasing week by week.' Pugh then referred to the construction of a proper hall seating a thousand people at a cost of two thousand pounds. He ended his article with a note of urgency:

The hall opened free of debt ... God help us to be up and doing—for we have only one short life to live and the opportunity for doing God's work will soon be over.

The work in East Moors continued to progress:

During the past months steady progress has been made and we have been much encouraged in seeing a goodly number accepting Christ as their portion ... prior to services, an open-air service is held and by this means we have been enabled to induce many to follow us to the Hall. We consider outdoor work essential to the success of our mission, for in this locality there are thousands who never enter a place of worship ... there is no other way of reaching them, but by taking the gospel to their doors.

Only three months later, we learn that:

Attendances have increased considerably and spiritual results have been most gratifying ... one Sunday 16 converts were received into fellowship ... several more converts are on probation ... note that our church, comprising 70 members now, is entirely made up, with only 4–5 exceptions, of men and women brought in from the world through the instrumentality of the Mission.

There is continued emphasis on the importance of open-air preaching, testimonies and singing:

More gospel action and Seth Joshua

Most of the success of our work is due to open-air meetings, held nightly prior to indoor services, and are well-attended by members who were rather bashful in going out into the streets, but they have been valiant soldiers of Jesus Christ. Such efforts have told in a remarkable way on the neighbourhood. Preaching and singing in the streets have had a most powerful effect in civilising and changing the spirit of the people, and we have had many instances of people coming to our Hall and deciding for Christ, who were first impressed while listening to us in the open air.

An example is given of one man who listened to their outdoor preaching several times but had never been inside a church for eighty-two years! He lived a careless life but now he is 'one of our happiest members and delights going out in the streets to witness for the Lord'.[12]

An editorial in the same edition reports of a significant change in Pugh's circumstances:

Most readers are aware that the Rev. John Pugh has resigned the pastorate Clifton Street Church to devote himself to evangelistic efforts in connection with Cardiff Evangelical Movement and to be free to respond to pressing calls from other fields for Mission services. He will leave his pastorate at the end of June (1892).

This decision was inevitable as Pugh's widening vision and burden led him to overstretch himself in taking commitments even outside Cardiff, as his advice and preaching were in demand by churches. Three months before resigning from his pastorate, in addition to extending the work in Cardiff, Pugh was preaching in places like Machynlleth in North Wales where he paid a five-day visit from the 11th–15th March, 1892. The services were held mostly in the English Presbyterian Church in the town centre and had been publicised well, with prayer meetings held for a week prior to Pugh's visit. We are informed that:

The Chapel was filled with a most attentive and appreciative congregation, with the hearers feeling that the gospel was fresh, as fresh as ever … a deeper interest

---

12 *The Christian Standard*, Vol. 1, No. 11, May 1892, pp. 4–5.

Chapter 8

was shown and larger gatherings were brought together and it was very clear that Mr Pugh's visit and his earnest and eloquent preaching were the themes of conversation in the town ... a few expressed the desire during the services to join the church of Christ. There are many ... whom we expect to see soon taking the same step.

Pugh preached the quarterly sermons at Whitefield Presbyterian Church, Abergavenny, on Sunday 4th February, and then friends

prevailed on Mr Pugh to stay with them on Monday and Tuesday to conduct mission services; considering the weather was so bad and no personal canvassing of the town had been made, there was a fair attendance and some souls were to decide for Christ ... Mr Pugh discovered a marked improvement here since the first and last times he had previously visited this church ...[13]

Llanidloes was another rural town he visited in mid-Wales, where in the English Presbyterian church John Pugh was 'an old familiar face and a welcome voice' where he had preached while a student in Trefeca, while for the younger members they knew of Pugh only by reputation until June 1891 when he visited the Association meetings there, and then in the August preached at the Anniversary services and again in January 1892, holding a week's mission:

During the third week of January, prayer meetings were held every night when fervent prayers were offered up imploring the blessing of Heaven upon the expected mission and it was felt that the earnest of the Spirit had been given. The weather was not good during the prayer meetings week so many did not attend, yet despite snow and frost the Master was very good.

Pugh arrived on Monday 25th January and there were a good number in the meeting that night. On Tuesday evening the congregation was 'considerably larger' and on the Wednesday 'the chapel was full', and by

---

13 *The Christian Standard*, Vol. 1, No. 9, March 1892, p. 8.

the Friday evening the meeting had to be held in the Congregational chapel where there was 'a splendid congregation' and two Mormon elders were present to the amazement of locals. On the Sunday night, Pugh preached to a congregation which was 'the largest known in the English chapel', but while only a 'few' gave themselves to Christ yet

many were strengthened and encouraged. Many were wounded ... never was there more powerful preaching.

On the Saturday afternoon, Pugh spoke in the local Spring Mill Factory when the workers, mostly young men and women, attended who had themselves asked for the service. He preached powerfully from 1 John 2:1: '... we have an Advocate with the Father, Jesus Christ the righteous':

John Pugh was at his best, quite at ease and his genial frankness and earnestness of purpose touched the hearts of the young people. They have all a tender and loving word for John Pugh.[14]

Requests for Pugh to preach in churches and hold missions increased while still developing the work in Cardiff and pastoring a church continued. A few weeks before he stood down as pastor in Cardiff, he was in Oswestry for a mission. Pugh had been there three years previously when he conducted 'a fortnight of special mission ... they all remember Mr Pugh so well ...'.[15] Concerning his visit in May 1892 we read that

Mr Pugh's preaching was very powerful and impressive. Weak mortals like ourselves naturally wonder how he can endure the strain and exertion ... His joyful spirit may perhaps be one secret of his power and his endurance. Whatever influences be at work about him, he is never seen to be depressed but is always cheerful and constrains others to be hopeful, cheerful and happy...

---

14 *The Christian Standard*, Vol. 1, No. 9, p. 10.
15 *The Christian Standard*, Vol. 1, No. 12, p. 10.

Chapter 8

John Pugh was an affable, kind person, sensitive to the needs of others, and his warm personality and confidence attracted people to him and to his preaching. His passion for the Lord's gospel to be preached and for people to be saved constrained him to work tirelessly, but the volume of work even in this early period began to affect Pugh's health. In October 1891, we read:

Owing to indisposition ... the Rev. John Pugh was not able to accomplish all he desired or fulfil all his promises during last month.

John Pugh told his old friends at Llanbedr that he was

extremely sorry to be unable, through indisposition, to preach for them on October 21st but he sincerely hoped that the Blessed Master was present, giving Professor Prys unusual power.[16]

His relentless labours for the gospel and longings for the unchurched to be saved made it difficult for him to refuse to preach when he saw needs and opportunities for the gospel. Despite his heavy workload, he always seized these opportunities. People wanted to hear Pugh and one reason was that he was 'a warmhearted and powerful preacher' of the gospel. His earnest appeals in preaching 'came from a heart burning with a desire to save souls'. He 'was imbued with the faith that moves mountains'. While he was not invited to many of the Welsh churches for special preaching occasions, the unchurched heard him gladly and responded.

Pugh needed more workers with the qualities of men like Seth Joshua and H. G. Howell. Greater prayer and financial support were also required. He himself needed encouragement as well as advice, but he desperately needed the support of churches and of the entire Presbyterian Church of Wales. Or should he work independently of his denomination? The needs were urgent. Pugh's vision was extensive. How did the Lord answer prayer?

That story continues in the next chapter.

---

16 *The Christian Standard*, Vol. 1, No. 3, September 1891, pp. 3–4.

9. 'Felt more like weeping'

'Go Forward' was the title of the front page article in the first issue of *The Christian Standard*[1] for July 1891. The name 'Forward Movement' was being used to refer to any special advance in Christian work and

> We cannot but see in all this the finger of God and that the Captain of the Lord of Hosts is in many ways repeating the command given of old: 'Speak to the children of Israel, that they go forward ...'. The work of extending our operations in Cardiff has been called already a 'forward movement'. We have not given it that name and have no desire to adopt it. New names ... become hackneyed and new methods stereotyped ... we have little desire for this movement, as a separate organisation ...

What follows in the article is a key argument and conviction of John Pugh concerning the history of the Presbyterian Church of Wales or, its earlier name, the Calvinistic Methodists:

> Welsh Methodism is pre-eminently a 'forward movement'. From that history we will draw our inspiration. In this sense, it is 'a backward movement'. We have to learn many a lesson from the founders of Methodism in the work of evangelising the masses. How elastic and adaptive were their methods ... We must, like them, preach the gospel which is for all times, with special application of it to the time

---

1 Vol. 1, No. 1, p. 1. *The Christian Standard* was the 'monthly magazine of the Cardiff Evangelical Movement', costing one penny. Its purpose was to communicate news of the evangelism in Cardiff and beyond being done by Pugh and colleagues under the new Movement. The name of the Magazine 'came to brother Pugh as an inspiration. Some of us wanted a more sectarian name but ... Pugh was right ... we have no desire to hoist the flag of a sect above the Banner of the Cross'. This Magazine was later renamed as *The Forward Movement Herald* from August 1897 but two years later changed to *The Forward Movement Torch*. The editor-in-chief of the latter was John Pugh from 1899–2006, with the exception of 1904. In 1913, this was incorporated in the denominational periodical, *The Monthly Treasury*.

Chapter 9

in which we live. In our efforts to reach the masses of our day, we must not be hampered by methods which were suitable in a by-gone age but now worse than useless anachronisms. Our denomination is distinctively an evangelistic body; if we adopt for convenience the name 'Cardiff Evangelical Movement' it is ... to emphasise the main feature of Welsh Methodism.

The message was clear. Pugh and his friends involved in, and supporting, the evangelising of the unchurched in industrial areas in particular were clearly in the tradition of their forefathers. The Rev. Matthews, Ewenny, had previously reassured Pugh of this fact when he started open-air preaching in his first pastorate in Tredegar, which had greatly encouraged the young evangelist.

Support

Formal and practical support from the Presbyterian Church of Wales for Pugh in reaching the unchurched was slow in being expressed and he felt some frustration, but there were encouragements on the way. News of how the Lord was blessing the work of evangelism in Cardiff and elsewhere filtered through in different ways to many churches throughout Wales. The mission in Cardiff was initially the work of one person, John Pugh,

who was overwhelmed with a deep sense of the spiritual destitution of Cardiff, and who felt that something out of the ordinary methods of the church was urgently needed.[2]

Pugh did not want to continue this work on his own or even under the name of a movement such as the Cardiff Evangelistic Movement which he had formed. He had a great love for his denomination, he loved its history and the biblical theology enshrined in its 1823 Confession of Faith. Furthermore, the Presbyterian Church of Wales had been born in revival and experienced many local and regional revivals during its subsequent

---

2 *The Romance of the Forward Movement*, pp. 72–81.

history. He was convinced, as we have seen, that the early leaders like Howel Harris, Daniel Rowland and others had responded in a similar way to the needs of the people in the eighteenth century.

Providentially, there existed within the Presbyterian denomination in Wales two societies with responsibility for evangelism. In North Wales there was 'The Home Mission Society' and in the South the 'English Causes Society' which Pugh himself supported and whose secretary was the energetic Rev. Lewis Ellis of Rhyl.

One highlight had been the General Assembly of the denomination held in Liverpool in 1890 attended by ministers and church elders who represented their various Presbyteries and Monthly Meetings. During the Assembly, a report was given from the 'English Causes Society' highlighting the disturbing number of towns in Wales where increasing numbers of people were not attending church. It was stated that the denomination should 'pay greater attention to mission work' in Wales. The Assembly agreed that one or two ministers should be released to devote their ministries to reach out in these towns to those neglecting church while a committee was appointed to monitor the situation further and consider the most appropriate ways of reaching the unchurched.

John Pugh attended this General Assembly as a delegate of the East Glamorgan Monthly Meeting, and during the discussion of the subject 'he unburdened his soul'. Emphasising the rapidly increasing population centres in towns and especially in industrial areas, he described the desperate moral, practical and spiritual needs of areas of Cardiff. Members of the Assembly were shaken by Pugh's moving speech.

In the 1891 General Asssembly in Morriston, Swansea, further progress was made when it was decided to establish the 'Church extension and Mission Work' with some tasked to explore further and arrange the provision of men and money for the work. The Assembly agreed that 'we greatly rejoice at the success of the new and strange enterprise commenced in Cardiff by the Rev. John J. Pugh and his helpers…'. This must have been a major encouragement for Pugh himself and his colleagues.

Chapter 9

Historic

There is no doubt that the **1892** General Assembly at Machynlleth was pivotal and historic because the denomination formally assumed ownership of the work Pugh had initiated. It was agreed that a Society should be formed and named 'The Church Extension and Mission Work' which would have three aims:

(a) To awaken the churches to their responsibilities, and to strengthen the hands of ministers and churches in difficult spheres;
(b) To enquire as to the number of those who neglect religious services in the populated areas;
(c) To establish mission stations wherever the needs for such arise.

It was also agreed that those

endowed with special aptitude for mission work be set apart, that they give their whole time and services to this Society.

Among the other decisions was the acceptance of the Movement in Cardiff and that

the Rev. John Pugh as a special missioner to give his whole time to the work of the Society.

John Pugh's reaction was one of joy:

The reception given to us when the kind Moderator, Dr W. Jones, called upon us to address the Assembly quite unnerved us, as we felt more like weeping than speaking. No sooner had we finished our address than Dr Charles Edwards jumped to his feet, and catching our hand with his two hands, said: 'I glorify God in you and I congratulate you for not saying too many or a word too few.'

Here at last was the assurance Pugh needed to continue his life work of mission within, and on behalf of, the Presbyterian Church of Wales.

A Forward Movement For Wales

Under the above title, news of the Assembly's decision and support was included in *The Christian Standard* the following month and with a note of excitement declaring that the

> great new Society called the 'Church Extension & Mission Work' to reclaim the five hundred thousand non-church young people now found in Wales, has been established by the General Assembly at Machynlleth and is now in active operation…[3]

The Assembly's decision was described as 'the greatest … for many years in the denomination' and 'statistics regarding the moral and spiritual parts of Wales are really appalling…'. The question was then asked: 'Are we equal to this…?' The answer given is that 'the great thing now is to … put ourselves in readiness and shape for prompt action'.

The article then drew encouragement as well as challenges from this major decision of the church. One encouragement was that the Cardiff Evangelistic Movement had been 'taken over in its entirety' and evangelists were now under the care and protection of the new Society with John Pugh being 'free to go to any place where there is found the greatest need, to stimulate towns and districts and open up new mission venues…'. However, there was a longing also 'to find other brethren moved and specially raised by the Lord to be set apart … for the thousands are perishing…'.

Readers were reassured that the work of mission is intended to 'stimulate all the existing churches in all our towns to turn out to do the work' because the new Society is 'not intended to do it apart from, or without, the present churches and their ministers, but through them…'. Reference was made to many 'earnest men and women, young and old, in our churches longing for more active service…'. Ministers were warned that they are responsible before God in this matter and it will 'be fearful if the people are not led on at once'. Finally, the need for prayer was emphasised.

---

3 Vol. 2, No. 1, July 1892, pp. 8–10.

Chapter 9

'God is with us'

John Pugh in his Report given in January 1894 was able to look back on the previous two years and claim that

> we stand today at a point of prosperity that even the most sanguine of us never expected to reach so soon. When we consider the Movement was only started a few months ago, and that in a very small way, and in one of the most hopeless parts of Cardiff, we have the greatest cause for thankfulness, and we take courage for it is evident that God is with us. The marvellous progress of the movement has been a source of great joy to us but ... we have met with great difficulties ... yet we believe that with faith in God, and pluck and perseverance, and a little sacrifice, the most difficult position in our line of battle may be captured for Christ and made a source of great blessing to any dark slum it may be near to.

Pugh reported that in response to 'earnest requests' from the Swansea District Meeting, he has promised to start a work in St Thomas, in the docks area of Swansea. Pugh wrote that

> We never thought there was a spot in Wales in such a plight. The great enemy of body and soul seems almost 'Monarch of all he surveys'...

Some churches had withdrawn from the area, but Pugh was ready for the challenge and also for the Western Valleys in Monmouthshire where, with a population of 252,000 at least, yet in all the county 'we only have approximately three thousand communicants...'. The Abercarn Centre had opened and in Six Bells the Centre ' promises well' and an evangelist was required for what is 'a needy place'.

Progress was also being made in the Rhondda Valley. As soon as a new coal pit was sunk and the coal worked, houses were built in the locality, but for English speakers there were no English services in churches except for Gelli, Ton Pentre, which had been established to meet the spiritual needs of English speakers. Over a period of five years the new churches in Tonypandy, Treorchy, Porth and Treherbert were becoming 'well established'.

The Tonypandy church grew considerably, having started with only eight members. Then five months later it had grown to forty members and met in a school before building a centre which soon became crowded. The Town Hall was used in December 1892 and preachers like John Pugh and Principal Prys preached powerfully to congregations of one thousand people over three Sundays. A large hall was going to be built to accommodate the large congregations.[4]

'Wales for Christ'

No time had been lost by John Pugh in continuing to share his vision and burden with churches and individuals. And his burden extended beyond Cardiff to the whole of Wales. In January 1892, therefore, Pugh had written an article with the arresting title: 'The Presbyterian Church of Wales: An Earnest Appeal for a Great United Action to Win Wales For Christ'.[5]

He needed the support of the entire denomination and argued his case:

There is no doubt that the crying need amongst us now is a mighty Home Mission Movement. The state of things in Wales and the Border counties calls loudly for the inauguration of a great, aggressive, evangelistic movement and for the adoption of new methods to cope with the changes ... Our church is the outcome of a great revival! It could be well for those who object to revivals to remember that the great Christian Church is the offspring of the mighty revival of Pentecost ... The great revivals of the church are the outcome of previous toil and suffering ... But, alas! Whilst we have been sleeping the wily and ever-wakeful foe has been sowing tares ... Every age has its own peculiar difficulties to contend with ... I suggest a new plan of campaign ... we change our present method of working. Churches are dying for lack of initiative. We cannot live on the past ... if people will not come to the church, let us adopt other means to reach them ... This is what our Methodist Fathers did. One practical suggestion is that men unqualified for the great work of the Christian Ministry should be urged to go back to their daily calling. Also, our Christian women should be utilised

---

4 *The Christian Standard*, Vol. 2, No. 20, March 1893, p. 3.
5 *The Christian Standard*, Vol. 1, No. 7, January 1892, pp. 9–11.

Chapter 9

more and more for the work ... They have been kept largely in the background and we are suffering today in consequence. And also give more prominence to great social movements which have the general good of the people in view ... Let us preach the same gospel and in the same Spirit as Daniel Rowland, Howel Harris, Thomas Charles, John Elias, John Jones (Talsarn), Henry Rees and Owen Thomas did. Let us pray for an outpouring of the Divine Spirit.

The message was uncompromising. The suggestions were in some respects radical and uncomfortable. Pugh was right in that the situation had changed significantly. Fewer people attended church and in the industrial areas the vast majority were ignorant of the gospel. The need was to go out to the people. The suggestion that unqualified men should not remain in the ministry was revolutionary. Churches were dying and new initiatives were required to reach people. Revival was a great need, but this did not relieve Christians and churches of their responsibility to toil for Christ, while at the same time there was a call to provide for the social needs of the people, a work in which women should be heavily involved. After all, this is how the Calvinistic Methodist church started and continued in the early stages. The challenge was an urgent one.

Other voices expressed the same need. For example, the Rev. D. M. Rees serving in the Gower area of Swansea wrote an article entitled 'The Forward Movement'.[6] Posing the question, 'In what sense are we to go forward?', he emphasised that

the first most needful step is for our churches to step out of the old methods adopted by our Fathers ... some are content with things as they are ... and deprecate any changes. But the separation of the people from the churches becomes wider and deeper so instead of helping the work of the gospel, the church blocks its way and impedes its progress. In many of our churches we want imagination; we are too stereotyped ... we must be ready to work through some venerable customs ... It must be borne in mind, however, that neither the church nor the individual soul can advance to spiritual conquests simply or chiefly by forging fresh weapons and tactics. The same

---

6 *The Christian Standard*, Vol. 1, No. 9, March 1892, p. 3.

'Felt more like weeping'

Spirit which possessed holy men of old must possess us ... To work for God is not optional, but imperative.

Were Christians being 'spoilt' in many of the churches? Rees warns that:

We are in great danger of spoiling Christians by doing too much for them. Our pastoral nurses feed them when they ought to be feeding themselves. We wheel them about in ecclesiastical prams when they ought to be strengthening their limbs by vigorous exercise ... They are perpetually devouring the finest of wheat and never doing Christian work.

The point being made was generally true with people in many congregations becoming sermon tasters, enjoying church life without sharing the gospel in their communities, and the point was enforced in the following way:

Jesus Christ did not spend His time in listening to sermons and enjoying the means of grace. He went about doing good. He sought the happiness of others. Every Christian must take an active part in the work. May we 'go forward'. Our prospects are bright ... they were never brighter, because they are as bright as the promises of a faithful God can make them ... If we are faithful ... God will bless our efforts to aid its triumphs and to some extent through our instrumentality. Wales shall be won for Christ!

A number of leaders agreed with Pugh and Rees and were taking action. One example is that of the Presbyterian churches in Rhyl, North Wales who

have lately formed a town Missionary Society and aggressive work for Christ has begun in earnest. A systematic visitation of the whole town has been undertaken and is being carried on. A mission station has been opened in the most neglected part of the town with very encouraging results.

And John Pugh had given impetus and support to this outreach:

Chapter 9

During the last week a fresh impetus has been given to the movement by the visit of the Rev. John Pugh, who has been holding a week's mission at the English Presbyterian Church. The congregations have been very good throughout the week, and there was an unction and a power about the meetings manifestly from on high … There are not a few who have been greatly blessed. The messages were clear, direct and powerful …

Pugh also had the opportunity of addressing the pastors and church elders in the Vale of Clwyd Monthly Meeting held in Rhyl during the mission when

he delivered an earnest and powerful address and the eyes of many Welsh ministers and officers were directed for the first time to the Cardiff Movement and their sympathies were strongly awakened. *The Christian Standard* was eagerly bought afterwards and back numbers taken. It was decided to invite John Pugh back as an Evangelist.[7]

Weeks later Pugh addressed the Quarterly Meetings of the Glamorgan, Monmouthshire and Carmarthenshire presbytery at Trinity Church, Aberdare. He reported that

as a result of the Cardiff Mission, three new churches had been constituted and received into the Connexion. Seth Joshua was received into membership and Mr Howells received as an evangelist and will be shortly examined with a view of being received as a preacher.

Presbytery would have heard of the mission in Builth Wells led by the evangelist H. G. Howell, now Cardiff based, from Monday 7th December to Sunday 13th December, 1891. Despite terrible storms which caused considerable destruction 'in our country which will be long remembered', yet:

Here it will be remembered as the time when God very clearly visited His people and brought to His church some who had for many years rejected the invitation. We had

---

7 *The Christian Standard*, Vol. 1, No. 7, January 1892, p. 12.

the great joy... seeing some old and young friends publicly declaring themselves to be on the Lord's side ... all felt that Mr Howell was indeed a man sent from God to us ... the Lord has done great things for us, whereof we are glad.

By March 1892, we learn that this Builth church

is in a very flourishing state ... a very cordial relationship exists between the pastor and his flock. The Sunday School is doing well ... there are some excellent young men in this church.

Many such encouragements were being received from across Wales, including a letter on behalf of the Church Meeting in Ebenezer, Haverfordwest:

I write to thank your Committee for releasing Seth Joshua in order to conduct special services here. Not since the visit of the Rev. John Pugh ten years ago has this town received such a blessing ... thirty-five people have been added to churches of the town.[8]

Not only did Pugh have these two excellent evangelists working with him, there was a stirring among some leaders and congregations to pray more while engaging in vigorous evangelism with the help of gifted preachers like Pugh, Joshua and Howell.

What about the Cardiff base and Pugh's own pastorate in Clifton Street? Again, there were some encouragements here:

Clifton Street, Cardiff—some of the most active members have thrown themselves heart and soul into the great movement (Cardiff Evangelical Movement) and are doing glorious service for their Master. But though Mr Pugh's time is occupied with the movement ... yet Clifton Street has held its own ...

---

8 *The Christian Standard*, Vol. 1, No. 9, March 1892, p. 11.

Chapter 9

Nevertheless, Pugh was being over-stretched and this was gradually being recognised, as evidenced at a meeting of the denominational Church Extension Committee where

the Cardiff Mission was favourably discussed. A desire was expressed to have similar missions started in populous districts. The Rev. John Pugh has been much pressed for a number of years to devote himself to itinerant mission work. The time is certainly ripe for the consideration of such an appointment.

Late June 1892, Pugh's role as Pastor of Clifton Street church ended and he was able to devote himself even more widely to evangelism. This, as we noticed, had received the recent approval of the General Assembly.

10. 'Grit! Grace! Gumption!'

The work in Cardiff continued to progress as new centres were opened. Clive Road is one example of a new centre located slightly West of Canton where an interdenominational Mission Hall had failed due to a lack of suitable leaders and organisation. This hall seating 350 was offered to Pugh for £470, so he immediately agreed to buy it, a decision later confirmed by the Glamorgan and Monmouthshire Presbytery in September 1891. The area surrounding the Hall was challenging and notorious but Pugh, unperturbed, welcomed the challenge.

J. E. Ray

Once again the Lord provided another suitable worker, this time to lead the outreach in Clive Road, Cardiff. His name was Mr J. E. Ray.

Ray's background is a thrilling one in that he had been greatly used in many different places before arriving in Cardiff. Born in Merthyr in 1863 and moving with his family at the age of nine to Treherbert in the Rhondda Valley, he was gloriously saved when 'a revival swept over the Rhondda' in 1879. Immediately he felt a call from God to give himself to Christian work. For approximately two years he was a faithful witness in his home area and was led to 'commence a work for God in Treforest' (near Pontypridd) where he used a Company's old shop as a mission room. A profound work of grace went on in the lives of men here and

many today regard that place as their second birth place. One remarkable feature of the work here in this out-of-the-way mission room was the number who seemed to get fitted with a desire for mission work and who afterwards became labourers in the vineyard, including Frank and Seth Joshua. The Holy Spirit elected to call out from an unknown work a number who have since become and still remain successful workers.

Chapter 10

Ray then went to Monmouth for a year where initially he was 'most severely tested' in being alone in the work and he endured much ridicule and persecution. Then he stayed for several months at a time in places like Coleford, Ludlow, Shrewsbury, and the latter was again 'a time of remarkable persecution' from people linked to the pubs. He and his wife needed police protection in going home from the services. After serving for a while in Scotland, they decided due to his wife's ill-health to go to Ipswich for three years where they served 'a most blessed work for God'. From Ipswich, they moved to Brighton, then North Wales, Stockport, Nelson (Lancs), Hertfordshire and Sydenham, each for several months at a time.

Reports of their work in England prior to arriving in Cardiff were most encouraging. In Ipswich

their labours have been much blessed and crowned with great spiritual success.

The Methodist Free Church minister in Ipswich, Rev. J. Fraser, shared his view of their work:

I have known much of his labours for the past two years in Ipswich and elsewhere, in which he has been used in bringing many souls to the Lord and the fruits of ministry are seen today ... he has shown a warm desire to promote the Lord's work outside of his own mission work and has rendered valuable service to my own circuit.

Their move to Cardiff involved them in serving Clive Road from the Autumn of 1891:

During the past nine weeks, they have laboured with much blessing, having endeared themselves to many hearts.

The words of the Rev. John Pugh are of even more significance:

I have known Evangelist Ray since he carried on a successful mission at Treforest in 1882. He was then very young ... but God wonderfully used him to the salvation of souls ... The Joshua brothers were brought to decide for Christ through the instrumentality of this humble lad from the Rhondda Valley. If these were the only fruit of his earnest efforts, it would have worth been living for, but Jonny Ray, as he was familiarly called by his friends, has been blessed to hundreds all over the land, and we are glad to have him join us ... in our efforts to win Cardiff and our fatherland for Christ.

Pugh now reports encouragingly on Ray's work in Clive Road:

During his short sojourn here he has been made a blessing to scores of poor perishing sinners. The work at Clive Road, Cardiff—under his charge since October 1891—has made great and substantial progress. This is now a church with nearly 100 members, a Band of Hope of 200 and a Sunday School with 250–300 ... Every department of the work in this important Centre is in a most flourishing condition ...[1]

A little later, it was reported that in 1892 over fifty new members were accepted, while some were placed on 'probation' which involved instruction, engagement in the work, observation concerning their lifestyle and the fruit of the Spirit in their lives.[2]

I have referred in more detail to Ray's work for several reasons. One is that Pugh was praying for suitable workers to engage with him in this aggressive form of evangelism to the unchurched. His prayers and those of others were being answered. Secondly, we note that the three men who had joined him in this early period were experienced and had been eminently fruitful and successful in their previous ministries. Thirdly, the three men were, like Pugh, burdened for evangelism, willing to sacrifice, suffer and work hard in the cause of the gospel. Fourthly, not one of these men had been through the recognised route of training for the ministry which obtained within the Presbyterian Church of Wales. Fifthly, they were spiritual men, pray-ers who depended on God for success and to whom the gospel of Christ meant everything. Finally, Mrs Ray had the

---

1 *The Christian Standard*, Vol. 2, No. 14, September 1892, pp. 1–3.
2 *The Christian Standard*, Vol. 2, No. 20, March 1893, p. 12.

Chapter 10

privilege of being appointed as the first lady evangelist under the Cardiff Evangelical Movement. She had been a great support for her husband in his ministry but had herself led missions and preached with some blessing on her work. After moving to Cardiff, she held missions in Pontypridd, North Wales, Dinas Powys ... Nantymoel and centres of the Cardiff Evangelical Movement. We are informed that

> At home, her preaching is very much appreciated. Her successful labours have forcibly impressed workers in Cardiff with the advisability of encouraging and utilising lady missionaries at home. It is hoped that many of our sisters will follow her example.[3]

In the same edition of *The Christian Standard*, there was an accompanying article referring to 'Female Ministry', but more widely there was an openness for women to lead missions and eventually take charge of Centres, with some raising the question of the possible ordination of women.

The need for more evangelists

The above was the title of an article written by John Pugh for *The Christian Standard* in March 1893. Despite having a handful of good evangelists, the need was so great and the openings for evangelism so many that more and more quality evangelists were required immediately. We need to appreciate the note of urgency as Pugh unburdens his heart here:

> One of the greatest difficulties is the want of suitable and adapted ministers or evangelists to enter on the work and to meet the crying need we have from so many districts in North as well as in South Wales ... we have had to go outside to other folks than our own in search of evangelists and to our amazement and sorrow none of our own ministers—young or old—appear yet to be so moved by the inspiration of the work ... and lay themselves out for the work among the masses.

---

3 *The Christian Standard*, Vol. 2, No. 15, October 1892, p. 1.

'Grit! Grace! Gumption!'

Pugh graciously acknowledges there may be genuine factors hindering some ministers from being involved in reaching the unchurched:

We cannot for a moment believe there is such a lack of spiritual life and responsibility among our students and pastors to debar them from the work ... ministers like others are disposed to get into a certain groove and it is very difficult to tear oneself away from the usual routine of becoming a pastor of our formed churches.

But there are serious questions which he posed, accompanied with the inevitable challenge too:

To keep up churches established a century ago, should not engross the whole energies of over one thousand ministers in our denomination ... What preparation is required? Do I have qualifications? What steps can we take to get into the work? These are some of the queries being raised.

Pugh answers some of the questions by indicating what is required of those who can be used as evangelists in the work:

Evangelists must be possessed with entire consecration to God and His work for better or for worse, have an aptitude for open-air preaching. And be ready to speak anywhere and with tact dealing with the degraded but with unction and power.

His final advice is given which included a strong confidence in God, the importance of prayer, but also practical steps which need to be taken:

First, God can create a minister anew for the occasion. Then the person should go and talk to Him and place oneself unreservedly in His hands—this is the all-important duty.

Second, all the facts and figures relative to the condition of the masses (outside the churches) should be placed in the hands of our ministers, students and our public generally ...

Chapter 10

Thirdly, we must all take this matter to God in prayer.

Concerning the first point, Pugh had seen the Lord do this in providing Seth Joshua, H. G. Howell and Jonny Ray, while the second step was being done in various ways with Pugh and his supporters beginning to publicise the need more regularly and challengingly. Finally, prayer for Pugh and his colleagues was foundational and they were now seeking to encourage more prayer in churches for the work.

Training

Pugh was determined to do something about training and it was an aspect which needed to be addressed by the denomination urgently, namely, the training of ministers and evangelists. Their training tended to be academic, although a little help was provided in terms of preaching. A University of Wales validated degree course of Bachelor of Divinity (BD) was introduced so that two students achieved the degree in 1900 from the University of Wales while another four students graduated in 1902. There was genuine and widespread appreciation[4] of the academic attainments of the six young ministers in obtaining the BD degree, but one fears that an overemphasis on the academic aspect of training was beginning to render ministers less able to identify with the working classes and communicate the gospel in ways they could understand.

Pugh, however, had his own immediate answer to the problem of training workers. In establishing the Cardiff Evangelical Movement in 1891 his aim was twofold. One aim was to establish

great mission centres to evangelise those who were at present beyond the pale and influence of all existing church organisations.

Related to that aim was a further essential provision, for he wanted to

---

4 '...the hallmark of wide knowledge and hard work': *The Monthly Treasury*, Vol. 3, No. 8, August 1902, p. 15.

set up a Training Home where Theological students training for the Ministry and also earnest young Christian, men and women, might have some *practical* knowledge of mission and pastoral work.[5]

However, Pugh was disappointed that his appeal for help met with 'no practical response', except from the previous Principal of Trefeca College.[6] He had 'great sorrow' over the matter and it was explained that:

...no part of his plan of campaign has been more commended than his idea of a Training Home ... yet all this has had is praise! Praise! Praise but without aid! But a Training Home cannot be built and furnished with beds and other necessities and supplies of food with simply praise ... A little practical help would be worth tons of empty praise. If those friends who admire this part of the scheme so much ... would put their shoulder to the wheel and get the funds for it, they would do a grand service for God and man.

Pugh had already identified a 'good site' and argued that a 'suitable house can be built for £500 which the ladies can furnish!' The impression given by Pugh was that he was

in dead earnest about it and that he is determined to give ministerial students all the benefit such a work as going on at Cardiff alone can give.

Pugh addressed the Trefeca and Bala College students on 12th and 14th May, inviting them to join heart and hand with evangelists during the coming summer vacation, promising he would provide 'secure boarding and lodgings ... during their stay'. Some younger men 'naturally jumped at such an offer and some older students would have done also'.

---

5   *The Christian Standard*, Vol. 1, No. 12, June 1892, pp. 2–3.
6   Principal D. Charles Davies, Trefeca, was enthusiastic concerning the proposal and promised financial help. He informed Pugh: 'I will gladly give you £30 per annum towards this training you propose having, for I believe it will supply the missing link between the Colleges and the churches, just as the hospital does between the medical student and his life work': *The Romance of the Forward Movement*, p. 95.

Chapter 10

'Grit! Grace! Gumption!'

This was the title of the address he delivered to the Trefeca and Bala students on this occasion and we need to follow his message closely, using his own words as far as possible:

… In Glamorgan and Monmouthsire, and in the West of England, the tug of war is being keenly felt … there the victory or death of the religious life of Wales will have to be settled … I have come to invite you to have a hand to hand fight with the foe and with all the forces of evil at his command. I am most anxious you should have all the benefits of the experience of those who have won it on the field of battle … the old methods of warfare will not succeed in the great centres, where the enemy is at his full force. If you are going to follow the old jog-trot-style of many you have watched, you will soon be left without much of a church or a congregation and your precious life largely wasted and lost. There is a need for practical training and a Home is also needed which the late Principal Davies(Trefeca) supported…

Following this introduction, Pugh then began to answer the question: 'What sort of men do we need?' His answer was given in those now well-known words—'Grit! Grace! Gumption!' We outline the three points as he developed them to the students:

1 GRIT

Before you can hope to do great service for God or much harm to the devil, you *MUST* have grit or moral stamina. A soft, flabby, goody-goody-baby of a fellow in man's clothes and a jolly sort of woman will never do much for God or harm the devil. I have never known of God using such people. Even a brave man when he gets into the dumps becomes useless and Elijah is an example … Do not run away with the notion that a gloomy countenance and a heavy heart is a mark of deep piety, for it is not. It is only a mark of sin or of a bad liver. 'The joy of the Lord is our strength…'.

It is the easiest thing in the world to frighten people with imaginary difficulties. Any mean coward can do that. But it takes a brave soul to inspire to noble deeds and Christ-like work. Young men … say to 'Little Faith'—be strong and labour valiantly for our people and for the cities of our God; for the Lord is with us: the God of Jacob is our refuge. We need to be brave!

2 GRACE

You must also have great grace! It is not enough to have grit and the gift of preaching. We must also have the *grace* of preaching. It is not enough to have the Holy Spirit abiding in us ... we must have the Holy Spirit resting upon us, overshadowing us, as the cloak of Elijah enveloped the person of Elijah.

Pugh then applied this aspect of grace in three ways: the grace of faith, the grace of hope and the grace which abounds in love. This powerful message deserves to be quoted directly, for it is deeply challenging for Christians in the twenty-first century:

(a) *Abound in the grace of faith*

Great faith is absolutely necessary before we can do any great work for God. All who have done great exploits for God and humanity have been mighty in faith ... (see Hebrews 11 but especially verses 33–39) ... But we ought to have more faith than any of these in Hebrews 11; for they lived in the dim past, whereas we live in the blaze of Calvary and of the Resurrection. When we look back and remember what Jesus Christ has done for our lost world, nothing should make us doubt. Have faith in God, in Christ and in the gospel. Whatever you do, don't air your doubts in the pulpits, for poor sinners are far more ready to doubt than to believe. I believe that one of the chief weaknesses of Welsh preaching has been to foster doubt regarding the question of assurance. Once you deprive a soul of assurance of personal salvation, through simple faith in Christ, you produce weakness instead of strength. Unbelief in ministers, like the unbelief of the ten spies, breeds ... moral cowards, who will never make a hole in the devil's kingdom. We must be able to say with Paul, 'I believe. Therefore have I spoken.' Oh, for a batch of ministers who, like Paul and John, kept ever ringing the charge, 'I know whom I believe.' Strong faith is essential to accomplish great things for God and man.

(b) *Abound in a mighty hope*

Your hope must amount to enthusiasm, to bear you onward in any great forward movement. Some people are very much afraid to be considered enthusiasts. I don't know why anyone should object to this, for it means that we are all ablaze in God and for God ... And there is everything in our work to make us burn with hopeful enthusiasm. We are engaged in a work that must succeed. Jesus Christ, whose we are and whom we serve, is bound to win for 'He shall see of the travail of His soul and be satisfied'. His death on the cross was not a speculation but a certainty. This fact should make us say, like (William Williams):

O'er these gloomy hills of darkness,
Look, my soul, be still, and gaze;
All the promises do prevail,
On a glorious day of grace.

Let the purposes and promises of God, let the Cross of Christ, let the Pentecosts of the past, and let the triumphs of the gospel in our land and other lands fill you with enthusiastic hope ... Don't be churchyard Christians—'For the sky, not the grave, is our goal' and victory is nigh for 'Christ must reign until every foe becomes His footstool'.

(c) **We must also abound in love:** 1 Corinthians 13.
All our gifts and all our accomplishments fall flat and worthless unless they are saturated with love for God and man ... You must get on the high platform of love before you can succeed in the service of God and humanity. Hence therefore the Lord's question to Peter in John chapter 21 was not, 'Do you now understand the nature of MY kingdom?' or, 'Do you understand clearly what I want you to do?' but rather, 'Do you love Me?' When Peter answered in the affirmative, He said: 'Feed My lambs ... My sheep'—the one great qualification is LOVE ... All the learning and all the eloquence will not make you a successful soul witness unless your soul is all ablaze with love to Christ and with love for people. But the vilest may be rescued ... in the spirit of love.

3 GUMPTION
Some people have plenty of moral stamina and a good share of grace but are very short of common sense ... which is most essential. But there is also a special wisdom needed for winning souls—'the wise win souls' and it is had through prayer, pondering and

practice. You can consider how others do it, folk like Spurgeon and D. L. Moody, but ... you must come and practise in the work itself.

In giving an annual report to the General Assembly of the Presbyterian Church of Wales, he confirmed the need for wisdom in the work:

One of the greatest needs of the times is of more men who possess the wisdom to win souls for Christ. Many excellent ministers there are in the land who could do a mighty work for God and country if they only knew how to use the power God has given them.[7]

John Pugh also preached in Trefeca College as well as delivering his address and we are told that he 'preached with his usual power and earnestness in the evening. The Memorial Hall was full'.[8]

We need to banish the idea that he was wanting an alternative path for training ministers. That was not so. His burden was that students for the ministry should receive *practical* training which would supplement the formal training received in Trefeca or Bala. There may have been defects in the formal training but Pugh wanted students to be actively involved in mission centres during the summer vacations in order to see what the Lord was doing and to learn themselves about evangelism to the masses outside the churches. That training would have involved daily morning worship, an address by Pugh or another evangelist, then in the afternoon visiting the homes of needy people and families. Early evening the students would be asked to preach in the open air and support the evangelist in the evening mission meeting. His plan of a Home for such training was not realised, although over the years several students annually took advantage of the scheme in one of the Mission Centres while given accommodation and meals. This was clearly beneficial to the students[9] and to the work itself as Pugh himself reported:

---

7 *The Romance of the Forward Movement*, p, 95.
8 *The Christian Standard*, Vol. 1, No. 12, June 1892, p. 4.
9 *The Romance of the Forward Movement*, pp. 96–98.

Chapter 10

We now use lodgings in private homes but this is a poor make-shift for a proper Training Home ... We can testify that those students who visited us during July and August that they greatly helped us in our great work and all of them testified that the visit had proved a mighty blessing to their own souls. Among the many blessings this work has brought us is the way it seems to influence our Divinity students. Does not this augur well for the future of our fatherland and all lands where these young men may be called in the providence of God to labour?

Pugh then expressed thanks to

the excellent Professors (in Trefeca and Bala) ... who encourage our students to pay us these visits, and especially Principal Prys for paying the board and lodging of three students for nine weeks of the vacation![10]

As the work expanded and the number of invitations increased for Pugh and his colleagues to conduct missions and open up new mission centres, the question became even more urgent: who would be called into the work? Pugh was desperately short of God-given evangelists.

In the next chapter, we will trace the rapid growth of the work and Pugh's role in it. His zeal for Christ and His gospel and reaching the unsaved and needy often overwhelmed him.

---

10 *The Christian Standard*, Vol. 2, No. 14, September 1892, p. 13.

11. An expanding work

The Rev. John Pugh was busy. Constrained by Christ's love and burdened to reach the masses of unchurched people, he worked tirelessly and unselfishly both locally and further afield, preaching, encouraging workers as well as supporters, identifying new sites and halls, then in addition opening up localities for gospel preaching. He overworked and found it difficult to refuse invitations to help churches or centres in challenging locations. A visionary and overwhelmed by the needs of unbelievers, Pugh not only preached Christ but lived supremely for Christ and His gospel. In this chapter we refer to examples of his heavy workload, then in a later chapter we will refer to his consequent health problems.

I remind you that we are not detailing the history of the Forward Movement but majoring on Pugh's personal involvement by providing examples of his work and the challenges he faced in this significant period of growth and expansion.

Cardiff

In March 1893, it was reported that in East Moors

... a large number have been led to accept salvation ... attendance at all the meetings has kept up wonderfully and is still improving ... On Sunday evening, January 26th, the Rev. John Pugh preached and his sermon, full of weighty matter, produced a very favourable impression on the audience, who listened throughout with an undivided attention ... 16 new members were received.[1]

Over a year later, 750 people were present in the evening service:

---

1 *The Christian Standard*, Vol. 2, No. 20, March 1893, p. 12.

Chapter 11

some brought in by open-air meeting prior to the service ... They listened well. The Master's presence was powerfully felt. At the close they held a prayer meeting and a large number remained and during prayers for conversions, a young man responded ... the prayer meeting continued and about to close when two more men responded in faith.[2]

Five years later, we are informed by a visiting minister that the services were

dignified and the gospel as pure and convincing in its delivery as anyone could desire ... Mr Howell was the pastor. The preaching here is of a thoroughly substantial character without any attempt at sensationalism.[3]

The standard of preaching and the reverence observed in all the meetings is worthy of note. Only a few weeks earlier, John Pugh had been in Liverpool attending the Monthly Presbytery:

After an address from Rev. Pugh on the Forward Movement, the meeting expressed its thankfulness for the excellent work done through Mr Pugh and his co-workers and urged the churches to exert themselves to increase the Forward Movement collection when the time arrives.[4]

In his six-monthly Report on the work up until late 1897, Pugh had

spoken of progress all along the line. At East Moors, Cardiff, 100 men 'had come out for Jesus in the course of a month and at Grangetown over 200 had sought salvation in the past six months'.[5]

The work in Grangetown, Cardiff, began in 1893 in a tent with Pugh himself leading the work. He also relocated his family to this area and

---

2 *The Christian Standard*, Vol. 2, No. 23, June 1893, p. 11.
3 *The Christian Standard*, Vol. 5, No. 49, January 1898, p. 12.
4 *The Christian Standard*, Vol. 4, No. 48, December 1897, p. 22.
5 *The Christian Standard*, Vol. 5, No. 50, February 1898, p. 25.

An expanding work

by the end of the first year there were 200 listeners and 52 adherents in the services; a temporary tin building was then used until a hall was built in 1895. Pugh was still leading this work at the end of 1897, helped by Mrs Pugh and daughters and a Mr Griffiths who are 'among its leading workers ... it is an active church ...'.

The pressure on Pugh was considerable and it is no surprise that while preaching a few weeks earlier in a mission in Liverpool[6] he 'broke down ... and has been recuperating in the Malvern area and is better'. Health issues would affect John Pugh increasingly over the following years due to overwork and the heavy responsibilities he shouldered.

Despite his health issues, gospel advance in Cardiff continued vigorously under Pugh's leadership. In addition to East Moors, Grangetown and Clive Road, other Centres were opened in Cardiff which included Canton, Saltmead, Cathays and Heath.

Pugh was especially concerned for the area of **Saltmead** as it was possibly the wildest and roughest area in Cardiff where gambling, prostitution and violence dominated. In 1895 a tent was set up for meetings, 'and it will be long remembered',[7] and then with increasing numbers of people attending, a tin building was used before a hall was opened in 1902. To meet the desperate social and physical needs of women in the area, a House for Friendless Women was made available in Saltmead during 1897, supervised by trained nurses and costing £100 per annum. The cry of Pugh and believers there was, 'Oh! For more simple trust in His goodness and power!'

Cathays involved a period of patient waiting for a suitable site, so it involved using a room initially, then different premises until a site was secured to build a large hall. During its erection, Pugh visited the site almost daily to monitor the progress and quality of the work![8]

Heath church was eventually started as a response to a deputation of mothers who visited Mrs Pugh while her husband was in the United

---

6 *The Monthly Treasury*, Vol. 2, No. 28, April 1896, p. 26.
7 *The Monthly Treasury*, Vol. 2, No. 23, November 1895, p. 15.
8 Today this is known as Highfields Church.

States[9] in 1900. The mothers were desperately concerned for the welfare and spiritual needs of children and adults in the Heath area. On his return, Pugh responded immediately by holding open-air, tent and house meetings in the Heath area. Prayer meetings were held regularly and Pugh quickly identified an ideal site on Whitchurch Road, almost opposite the Army barracks, where a Hall would be built accommodating four hundred people; this was opened in early November 1901. There were extensive efforts beforehand to evangelise the entire area, involving visiting each house. By late January 1901 there were as many as 18 believing members enrolled and the church was functioning in the district.

Wales

While establishing and caring for Centres in Cardiff, Pugh's ministry was extensive and in demand in all parts of Wales. The last week in February 1892 he led a week's mission in **Holywell**, Flintshire, in the English Presbyterian church where packed congregations listened 'with rapt attention'[10] to his preaching. Frequently he participated in induction and commissioning services for pastors and evangelists. In **Ynysybwl**, Pontypridd, for example, the Rev. T. Evans was inducted on 13th June, 1892 as Pastor when Pugh led the devotions, including 'a fervent prayer for the blessing of God on pastor and church'. Later in the service, 'in a telling speech he dwelt upon the duty of the church to support its minister in various ways'. How should this be expressed? By prayer, faithful attendance and expressing appreciation for his ministry. He then challenged the church that their pastor:

'had a body and soul much like their own, and needed support and sympathy, as much as they did … God had not sent an angelic being among them … he must be clothed and fed with his family needing the same things. If Mr Evans worked amongst them

---

9 He was a delegate to the Pan-Presbyterian Congress at Washington. Rev. J.Cynddylan Jones had also recommended that during his three-month stay in America he should represent the South Wales Quarterly Association. That was agreed unanimously: *The Monthly Treasury*, Vol. 6, No. 69, September 1899, p. 21.

10 *The Christian Standard*, Vol. 1, No. 10, April 1892, p. 5.

as he had worked elsewhere in the past ... they would see the blessing of God on the cause at Ynysybwl...'[11]

Pugh thought highly of the new pastor and had known his wife from childhood.

A few weeks later Pugh was preaching in the **Porth** centre, the gateway to the Rhondda Valley, then in the young church at **Graig**, Pontypridd. The latter church felt its 'inability to evangelise the seething mass of degraded humanity around them' and appealed to Pugh who immediately consulted neighbouring churches in an attempt to provide united support for the church. A large hall was hired for Sunday services and Pugh preached to 'large congregations' while the Graig Hall was used for children's meetings and Sunday School. The church 'felt that there was hope still for the Graig district which has ever been looked upon as the most hopeless spot in the district'.[12] The young church together with that in Porth were placed by the East Glamorgan Monthly Meeting 'under the charge of John Pugh'.

In October 1892 Pugh was back in **Tredegar** preaching in a five-day mission in his former church. Pugh was delighted 'to hear ... there were signs of blessing ... which years before had witnessed the mighty works of God'.[13] A dozen young men had been converted prior to Pugh's visit with even more entering the kingdom during the week of prayer, days before the mission started. Under Pugh's powerful preaching, more young and elderly folk were saved. John Pugh was greatly encouraged during this mission and time was taken to reflect on his earlier ministry in Tredegar when 'the Lord was present'. Pugh's only faith was

in personal contact with the personal Saviour! This he feels is the one need of sinners. And anything short of this, will not affect a perfect cure, all else is only patchwork; Christ FOR man and Christ IN man, is the only remedy ... for the ills of people. Pugh only promised to stay at Tredegar for five years but owing to the ... strike, he declined a tempting call and remained another four years. Some hundreds were gathered into

---

11 *The Christian Standard*, Vol. 2, No. 1, July 1892, p. 3.
12 *The Christian Standard*, Vol. 2, No. 17, December 1892, pp. 12–13.
13 *The Christian Standard*, Vol. 2, No. 16, November 1892, p. 7.

Chapter 11

various churches through his open-air services in nine years and his own church received some additions continually. In January and February 1879, as many as 72 were added to the church in six weeks. Scores of young men were saved but left for work, some emigrated to America or the colonies ... but the good news was that they were living in Christ and that used to cheer us greatly ... He still carries on the work for this part of the vineyard which has never looked better than now!

Almost immediately Pugh had gone with one of his colleagues to Abercarn to conduct a six-day mission and the report is encouraging:

A spirit of revival has taken place in the church of late ... Its history over the past fifty years has been one of hard struggle and patient perseverance by a small group. The members now are mostly young people ... since the advent of the Rev. Davies three years ago, the meeting place has become inadequate and was enlarged in August 1891.

The meetings held by Pugh and his staff

have been a source of great blessing to the church and neighbourhood and up to the Wednesday of that week over twenty had decided for Christ.

In April 1893, Pugh preached at eight meetings during the week under divine blessing. A new mission hall was opened on February 11th, 1894, then later on the 25th of the month John Pugh preached three times and in the evening formed the Centre formally into a church.[14]

Demanding schedule

The Forward Movement Notes[15] for January 1893 provide further insight into the demanding schedule and itinerary facing John Pugh on a regular basis. Pugh 'arrived in Cardiff just in time' early January to meet the Sub-Committee of the Forward Movement. The next day he was in Briton Ferry for the West Glamorgan Monthly Meeting where he gave an account

---

14 *The Monthly Treasury*, Vol. 1, No. 4, April 1894, p. 17.
15 *The Christian Standard*, Vol. 2, No. 19, February 1893, pp. 10–12.

An expanding work

of developments in the Forward Movement. When he started, he described how the work started in an old tent in Cardiff, referring to the

> marvellous things which God had done for them, but he was so overcome that he failed to proceed for some time; he seemed so overwhelmed with the magnitude of God's goodness to him and the men who were engaged in the great movement, that he utterly broke down and could not go on for weeping.

After this meeting, he went to Swansea to meet the local committee regarding the witness in St Thomas in the docks area of the town. He preached and the meeting 'was just as remarkable for the Divine presence as in the afternoon…'. A train journey to Abergavenny was scheduled for the following morning to attend the Glamorgan and Monmouthshire Presbytery Quarterly Meeting, and then accompanied by the Rev. Lewis Ellis they travelled by train to Abertillery where they spent the night with an ardent supporter of the work before exploring further the needs of the Western Valleys so familiar to Pugh. Ellis saw the entire area as

> a new world as he witnessed great towns springing up like mushrooms and scarcely any religious provision made for them … he seemed perfectly amazed and wished his North Wales friends could have one glimpse of the sight.

In Abercarn they called to see two 'ardent supporters' who warmly welcomed them, and then they travelled to Cross Keys which was the first Forward Movement Centre 'in these great Valleys'. They were met by evangelist Jackson

> whom God had so greatly blessed and made instrumental to bring about a mighty change in this beautiful and rising district…

They travelled home to Cardiff for the night and Porth and then Pontypridd were the towns they visited the next day, despite heavy snow showers. This is a small indication of the demands on Pugh's time and energies. Committees, Presbytery meetings, buildings and finance, encouraging

Chapter 11

supporters, preaching, conducting missions over several days in various places and caring for workers while at the same time exploring new areas for gospel advance were all part of a regular routine for John Pugh.

Guidance had been given to Pugh by the newly formed Church Extension and Mission Work Society at its first meeting in Chester in August 1892. After receiving news of the work from Pugh and colleagues, four formal but practical steps were agreed:

first, while sympathising with the calls for mission work from many places ... we think it wise in view of the present state and resources of the Society, to use every means to develop and establish causes in the great populous districts where the need is desperate; **second,** in expressing joy at the success in the great work in Cardiff, we adopt the following places as centres of operation from which surrounding neighbourhoods will be worked—East Moors, Cowbridge Road, Clive Road, Swansea, Porth, Western Valley; **third,** that the Executive Committee with John Pugh and the County Committee look out for missionaries for the above places and, **fourth,** a stated salary be paid to John Pugh.[16]

The latter provision was urgent as Pugh's salary needed to be clarified and confirmed. The third step would have heartened Pugh as they would share the burden in identifying workers for these centres, although too often it was left to Pugh himself who knew only too well the qualities required in men to lead such aggressive evangelism to the unchurched. The first two steps were wise, especially using new Centres as platforms for further advance. Caution was being advised in the kindest manner, but Pugh's burning love for Christ and people, the incessant appeals from churches and areas for help, coupled with the glaring needs of the socially needy and populous areas, meant that Pugh found it difficult to refuse to initiate work in new areas. However, with regard to the Western Valleys and the invitation of friends there, Pugh visited the area and friends—as we have seen—to identify places 'where Mission centres could be opened'. The result was in line with the above practical steps:

---

16 *The Christian Standard*, Vol. 2, No. 15, October 1892, pp. 11–12.

An expanding work

The state of many of these places is truly deplorable and it is hoped that mission campaigns to be held here will be prosecuted vigorously.

Following Pugh's death in 1907, *The Monthly Treasury* reported that

in Monmouthshire, the population is increasing so fast ... neither church nor state can cope with such a growth ... there are openings for new causes in 12 places—some large towns or villages like Blackwood and we do not have a single church there. Also there is Rhymney with our three Welsh churches but the need is for an English church there ... resources are not enough and 12 new causes would overwhelm Presbytery. One of the twelve causes has started in Glannant, Pengam and the Forward Movement expressed readiness to start a cause at Rhymney ... only a beginning. Within the next twelve months, some real hard work has to be done ... Monmouthshire is worth saving. The railways are fighting a tremendous battle for the right of carrying coal and are spending thousands of pounds ... Surely we ought to be prepared to spend money and men in order to win souls for Christ and the church. Shall the railway companies be more zealous than ourselves?

In the spirit and language of John Pugh, this report proceeds to employ the historical and theological arguments used so effectively by Pugh on occasions:

Howel Harris lost blood in Monmouthshire. Morgan Howell spent his energy in and for Monmouthshire. The dust of Islwyn sanctifies the soil of Monmouthshire. The past is rich.

The pressures on Pugh were considerable and increased monthly as new challenges were presented to him and he found it difficult to refuse help if the need was great.

Examples of further ways Pugh responded to these needs will be provided in the next chapter.

12. '... In labours abundant...'

Alongside the encouraging evangelistic and church planting work proceeding in Cardiff, Pugh had a growing concern to develop gospel work throughout Wales, especially in key towns which included **Swansea**. A local committee in Swansea met with Pugh in 1892 to ascertain what steps could be taken to evangelise the town. Typical of Pugh's approach, action was taken swiftly and 'services commenced in a tent pitched at Rhydding's Field on 7th August 1892'.[1] Seth Joshua preached on the first Sunday and Pugh also visited occasionally to preach there. In less than a year, Rhydding's Hall was opened when among ministers officiating was John Pugh who did so 'with considerable heartiness and unction...'.[2]

A further development was the handing over to the Forward Movement of Hebron Welsh Chapel in the docks area of St Thomas, Port Tennant: 'It was felt something ought to be done for St Thomas and in English.' Initially this involved more work for Pugh. Hebron had been a problem church with its lack of unity and ineffectiveness in a needy area. The first action taken by Pugh was to remove all nominal members of the old church and start afresh with a new church and membership with the insistence that all members should be total abstainers. On Sunday 9th October (1892), Pugh

conducted three services; he had good congregations afternoon and evening as well as every evening of the following week. There is a mighty work for God to be done in this neglected part of Swansea.

---

1 *The Christian Standard*, Vol. 2, No. 14, September 1892, p. 10.
2 *The Christian Standard*, Vol. 2, No. 23, June 1893, p. 16. The opening took place between the 7th to the 19th May, 1893.

'...In labours abundant...'

Pugh felt that a local evangelist by the name of Rees

seems especially qualified for the area ... he has already found great favour with the people.[3]

Six months later 'difficulties and challenges'[4] were reported in St Thomas, which was not surprising, but after considerable efforts to evangelise from the old Hebron church building, the work was relocated to a new tin building in Port Tennant and a week's mission was held in February 1896 led by Mr and Mrs J. E. Ray and there were 'many conversions'. Three years later a Trefeca student, William Meredith, began ministry there and

the church rapidly grew in congregation and membership ... that necessity impelled the growing church to venture on a larger and more permanent building...[5]

In 1897, an evangelistic work was launched in 'a dark and much neglected spot' nearby in the adjoining Burrows where again the gospel prevailed in many lives there. Pugh, with his business acumen and alertness, also identified an ideal building for sale in the centre of Swansea which became available at a reduced price and would seat 1,500 people. The building was purchased and named Central Hall which opened in February 1906 with Seth Joshua appointed as the evangelist in charge who reported:

The conversion of the people began on the first day, and since then we have seen a constant stream of blessing.[6]

Other Centres were opened in the Swansea area but Pugh was concerned also for the key town of **Newport** where again he used Seth Joshua, helped by his brother Frank while on holiday in August 1895, to

---

3 *The Christian Standard*, Vol. 2, No. 16, 1892, p. 7.
4 *The Christian Standard*, Vol. 2, No. 22, May 1893, p. 14.
5 *The Romance of the Forward Movement*, pp. 116–117.
6 *The Romance of the Forward Movement*, pp. 118–119.

Chapter 12

initiate evangelism there. They advertised extensively their presence and the meetings to be held in the Temperance Hall with many listening to the gospel preaching there. Within a year, about a hundred people had professed faith in Christ and a church was constituted. In the Malpas area of the town, a large hall was opened in 1897 for pioneer evangelism. To their relief, a good congregation met there and within five months there were thirty members.[7] Between 1894 and 1907 when Pugh died, the number of Presbyterian churches in the town of Newport increased from two to eight with 1,600 members and as many as 5,000 hearers.

Reports

Regular and formal reports to denominational meetings provide insight into the development of the work and the pressures but also excitement Pugh felt during the 1890s. In **April 1893,** he reported that

1) 'Mission work is growing with wonderful rapidity ... many new Centres ... also the vast numbers of outsiders who crowd the halls on Sundays and week evenings. There are over 1,000 attending Porth Hall and 900 in East Moors, Cardiff. There are 4 Centres in Cardiff, 2 in Swansea, Centres in Porth, Graig (Pontypridd), Cross Keys, Abertillery and Abercarn. Evangelists are stationed in most of these Centres.

2) The process of consolidating goes on most satisfactorily with excellent provision to watch over and assist in carrying on the work in the Cardiff area by the United Committee of the West & East Glamorgan, Monmouth Presbytery meetings.

3) Sympathy and enthusiasm for Forward Movement work 'seems to have taken possession of the whole denomination'.

4) The thank-offering during the Week of Prayer proved a success.

The Report then draws attention to

---

[7] *The Romance of the Forward Movement,* pp. 113–118.

a vast amount of work already accomplished in the short space of less than two years. The present evangelists appear to be sent by God to us. They work hard, so hard they are nearly worked off their feet ... Many things are urgently needed ... Above all things more evangelists prepared and sent by God, but trained by ourselves ... so need of a Training Home in Cardiff.[8]

A letter was made available concerning this work which was intended to be read in all the churches of the denomination on the first Sunday in **1898** and it included the following details:

There are now 30 churches established under the auspices of the Forward Movement in 1896 with 10,486 adherents, 1,539 Communicants, 789 children and 4,676 Sunday School scholars. Some of the churches were only recently started, especially the Newport Centres and Wrexham. The money which is needed for grants to the Centres is approximately £3,000 per year.[9]

Three years later (1901) Pugh reported to the General Assembly:

The growing need for new centres to meet the increasing population in South Wales ... a large Fund needed to meet this ... the work in the Temperance Hall, Newport was self-supporting and other Centres urged to do the same ... urged its claims on the continued support of the denomination ... Everyone must feel the need of a great Revival. The materialism of this age is sapping the life-blood of our people in great centres of population. There are more practical Pagans in Wales and Monmouthshire today than when God called Howel Harris and Daniel Rowland to evangelise ... we are helpless for lack of funds to extend our mission so suggest a Self Denial Week 27th October – 3rd November.[10]

John Pugh received regular encouragement, for a few weeks earlier the question was asked in *The Monthly Treasury*:

---

8 *The Christian Standard*, Vol. 2, No. 22, May 1893, pp. 12–13.
9 *The Monthly Treasury*, Vol. 5, No. 49, January 1898, p. 13.
10 *The Monthly Treasury*, Vol. 2, No. 10, October 1901, p. 13.

Chapter 12

Are we progressing? ... Yes, in Cardiff twenty years ago there were five Calvinistic Methodist churches in the Borough (three Welsh and two English) but now there are five Welsh and ten English churches with two branches. At the end of 1881 the total number of members was 742 but by the end of 1890 there was a three-fold increase to 2,413 members ... The Forward Movement is 'the chief factor'.[11]

This was welcome encouragement for Pugh which was underlined biblically by the retiring Moderator[12] in the North Wales Association meetings in Colwyn Bay in the same summer. He spoke on 'The Mission of the Connexion in the New Century', emphasising that

...the saving of the people ... was our Father's mission and also must be ours. This is our raise d'être...'

By early 1904, the Rev. Barrow Williams also claimed that

After twelve years ... the success (of the Forward Movement) has been notable with 41 Stations and 5 Branches and in North Wales 5 Stations and 1 Branch ... Having visited many of the 'Centres', I can personally testify to the greatness and thoroughness of the work done by the Evangelists and their wives. The influence of the Forward Movement on the whole denomination has been most healthy ... Nowadays the Connexion has become very respectable and some fear it would become 'ULTRA-respectable' and lose its hold on the masses.[13]

While appreciating the advances made over previous years and the new churches established, a year later Pugh remained overwhelmed by the continuing population increase in the South Wales industrial areas, but he was not in despair:

...The population of South Wales is increasing ... we ought to strive to keep pace with this fast growth of population and provide for the spiritual needs of the people

---

11 Vol. 2, No. 6, June 1991, p. 14.
12 Rev. Evan Roberts, Dolgellau.
13 *The Monthly Treasury*, Vol. 5, No. 1, January 1904, p. 8.

… We have the machinery ready but we lack the means to carry on and extend the work … The Lord has been very gracious to Wales during the past twelve months and thousands have seen their Redeemer … the work to be done is so great that we are in danger of being frightened and disheartened. Our faith is being put to the test … but 'things which are impossible with men are possible with God'.[14]

When addressing his Presbytery in the Autumn of 1897, Pugh continued to plead with members 'to be alive' to the religious needs of the locality and referred as an example to the Crwys estate in Cardiff, and as a consequence a small committee was appointed to select a site for a church building. Probably more than anyone else, Pugh was aware of the need facing the church in reaching the unchurched.[15] Four weeks later at a Forward Movement meeting on the eve of the Swansea Conference, Principal Prys emphasised the important role of the Movement, stating

he heartily believed that the Almighty God took possession of Mr Pugh and showed him that the Christian Church of Wales did not do its duty. When the church was warm in the heat of its first love, the church in Wales expanded and stretched forth its hand to the world; but when it lost its first love, it became contracted, leaving the masses in its interest for the middle classes. It became an eminently middle-class institution. But the Forward Movement appealed to all classes … like an advance guard sent on in front in order to show the whole army in which direction to go. The Forward Movement had realised that every man and woman is worth saving…[16]

In God's purpose, John Pugh was the man who sought to mobilise the army with a profound love for Christ and people, especially the unchurched. God had taken possession of Pugh and Calvary love constrained him in all he endeavoured to do.

Reviewing the work for the benefit of the General Committee at its half-yearly meeting in December 1898, Pugh shared that

---

14 *The Monthly Treasury*, Vol. 10, No. 12, December 1905, p. 26.
15 *The Monthly Treasury*, Vol. 4, No. 46, October 1897, p. 26.
16 *The Monthly Treasury*, Vol. 4, No. 47, November 1897, pp. 4–6.

Chapter 12

no new congregations have been formed ... Forward Movement churches suffered greatly during the Great Strike of 1898 but providentially the Centres have held on their way ...[17]

Pugh is referring to the Welsh coal strike which continued for six months from early April 1898. The strike was a failed attempt to remove the sliding scale payment system linking salaries to the price of coal on the open market. Miners argued that the scale could be exploited by traders and owners to the detriment of the miners themselves; this strike contributed to the emergence of trade unions in Wales and the formation of the South Wales Miners' Federation. Confirming the impact of the Strike on the young churches and Centres, the same issue of the Magazine included Principal Edwards's Annual letter and Appeal to churches for the Forward Movement which stated:

... Many of the Causes already established have just emerged from a severe crisis and many are in a lamentable condition financially. This tends to dishearten workers and to injure the work ...

Nevertheless, the Lord was both extending the work and preserving it despite the 1898 strike. Pugh's heart must have been warmed and delighted to hear of considerable blessing in churches like Merthyr Vale two years prior to the strike:

A great awakening has taken place at Merthyr Vale. Revival meetings, prayer meetings and open-air meetings have been held and the churches are reaping the fruit of their labours. The English church has had several additions to the membership and at the Aberfan Welsh church the movement has reached high tide. On Thursday evening, members had assembled for their church meeting, but so unusual was the attendance that they had to sojourn from the schoolroom to the chapel, when it was discovered that 35 'strangers' were present under conviction and anxious to join in Christian fellowship. The 35 people were cordially welcomed ... The church

---

17 *The Monthly Treasury*, Vol. 6, No. 61, January 1899, p. 24.

and congregation at Aberafon are amongst the most flourishing in the county and the faith of those who, fifteen years ago, ventured upon so large a chapel, has been amply rewarded.[18]

The same year a layman, Mr A. T. Roberts, addressed the Bala Students Literary Society under the title of *A Case For An Aggressive Missionary Policy*. He represented a growing number of leaders within the denomination who supported Pugh's vision of reaching the unchurched in populated areas. 'Virgin soil is best,' he affirmed, 'and fishermen go where there are fish'! He continued:

A first condition of growth is to grow ... It is to the Church's interest today to work especially in large towns and new growing districts. Our denomination needs to mark this. The best paying investment ... is undoubtedly the Forward Movement.

Pugh had been saying this for several years, so this confirmation in print must have been music to his ears. On the other hand, the speaker reminded the Bala students that Pugh's Forward Movement was not alone or unique in reaching the heavily populated industrial areas of Wales with the gospel. He referred to the Baptists in Wales who were increasing at five times the rate of the Primitive Methodists in England and Wales. One reason he gave for this statistic is that

Primitive Methodists work chiefly in rural areas and the areas are being depleted, while Baptists, largely in Glamorgan and Monmouthshire, work in the most rapidly growing areas of Wales.[19]

The principle also applied world-wide, but John Pugh therefore was not alone in the burden he felt or in the emphasis he placed on reaching the most populated areas in the industrial landscape. While Pugh may have been the outstanding leader in this outreach, there remained industrial

---

18 *The Monthly Treasury*, Vol. 2, No. 27, March 1896, p. 6.
19 *The Monthly Treasury*, Vol. 2, No. 28, April 1896, p. 7.

areas in Wales outside Glamorgan and Monmouthshire where there was no or little evangelism.

North Wales

Passionate appeals were made by churches in North Wales to do something similar in their areas or, at least, to conduct evangelistic services and encourage their churches to reach out to the unchurched. Pugh was surprised by their earnest and persistent appeals and it was only after some considerable time that he felt free to respond. The initial step was to send evangelists like Seth Joshua, H. G. Howell and Mr and Mrs Ray 'to spy the land and meet the local committee' on their 'missionary journeys through the North'.[20] They were encouraged to lead missions and stir both Welsh- and English-speaking churches to their responsibilities for evangelism. The most urgent and pressing appeals to Pugh had come from Wrexham where coal mining had developed rapidly, making Wrexham the largest town in North Wales and at the heart of the burgeoning coal industry there. Support was given to Pugh and the Forward Movement in this venture, and then in 1898 the Rays were released to open the mission in Wrexham. Pugh himself was involved in preaching on occasions and monitoring the progress of the work in the North. In January 1998 it was reported that the

Rev. John Pugh has returned to Cardiff after his Forward Movement work in Wrexham and district ... Mr Pugh conducted a large number of meetings...[21]

Other evangelists also visited the Wrexham area periodically for missions. Seth Joshua had been recognised as Connexional Evangelist from 1904 and travelled widely in that capacity, including preaching at a week's mission in Wrexham from 13th–20th March. His diary entry is very revealing:

---

20 *The Romance of the Forward Movement*, pp. 124–127.
21 *The Monthly Treasury*, Vol. 5, No. 49, January 1898, p. 25.

'...In labours abundant...'

I am very anxious about this mission, and can only lean on the divine strength for all help. The circumstances there demand much wisdom, caution, and self-control. I shall need to be self-contained and to withdraw from the external in order to find a secret pavilion.[22]

Here is a reminder that he and other evangelists in this period, including Pugh, attached major importance to prayer and depending believingly on the Lord for success in their ministries.

More of this later, but we now turn to John Pugh and his travels outside Wales, some of which were enforced due to illness and exhaustion.

---

22 *Seth and Frank Joshua*, p. 66.

13. Scotland and Wales

While Pugh's vision and burden extended beyond Cardiff and south-east Wales to the whole of Wales, he also travelled regularly to Scotland, as we noted in an earlier chapter.

Pugh's daughter had no hesitation in affirming that the Rev. William Ross, the Scottish Free Church of Scotland minister, was her father's 'bosom friend' and the facts point to a close relationship between the two men. They were of a kindred spirit with the same burdens and vision.

The relationship began early in Pugh's ministry in Tredegar when he visited Ross when he ministered on the Isle of Bute in Rothesay. Pugh had the privilege of preaching in a mission there. When Ross moved to the Cowcaddens church in Glasgow in 1883, Pugh visited his church almost annually, while Ross himself frequently visited Wales. Ross's support for Pugh and his ministry in Wales were greatly valued. They were a mutual support for one another. Pugh's chief purpose for visiting Glasgow regularly was to preach in the church's regular seasons of evangelistic meetings, where his preaching was greatly appreciated and welcomed.

There was nothing attractive about the Cowcaddens church when Ross went there. There were only one hundred members at the time, no comfortable manse, and the church building had a debt of £5,000. The area too was socially deprived. While considering going to the church, an evangelist told Ross:

Don't go to Cowcaddens. I know it well. The mass of people are mostly tenants and probably the majority are Roman Catholic. The population is constantly shifting ... They are very poor and between theatres, pubs and other influences, multitudes are degraded. Without exceptional means, of which you have not the command, not much of a permanent character will ever come out of the Cowcaddens. Think before you go![1]

---

1 *The Christian Standard*, Vol. 2, No. 18, January 1893, pp. 1–3.

Scotland and Wales

On the evening of Saturday 20th October 1883, Ross surveyed the district carefully and felt that the burden of the work needing to be done there was intolerable. In all his fears and doubts, suddenly 'a voice seemed to say: "I have much people in this city."' And to 'a whole-souled servant of Christ', the district was not without its attraction. As Ross commented:

The field is ample to satisfy the largest ambition. The degradation of the people was thorough.

The debt-ridden building was no deterrent to Ross either while he appreciated there were eight devoted office bearers. He now heard of the pioneer work which had already been done in the neighbourhood, for D. L. Moody had made the church the centre of his labours in the north of Glasgow during his mission in 1882. Then after Moody left, the United Evangelistic Association continued the work until the end of 1883. These facts served to confirm that the Lord had called him to Cowcaddens, so he accepted the call.

His future evangelistic work in the area was to be accomplished through this local church with meetings being held nightly. Various agencies were started with conversion as the immediate end in view, and open-air meetings were to be held daily, especially before meetings. Prayer was also emphasised as an expression of dependence on God for spiritual success. Ross felt that the children had been sadly neglected and provision was made for them to know the Bible and understand the gospel. Temperance was also important to this new minister, but so also was the equipping of women for social and medical care in the parish and teaching the Bible to ladies. The developments in the work were enormous and wide-ranging but geared to the social and spiritual needs of people in the area. During the first four years of his pastorate in Glasgow, 1,250 members had joined the church, the majority of whom had been rescued from the depths of sin and social deprivation. The church debt of £5,000 'was soon wiped away'.

This work and Ross's motivation would have greatly encouraged John Pugh on his regular visits there. Their hearts were knit together

Chapter 13

in this basic but demanding gospel work prompted by a deep love of Christ and of people. The two men were also similar in temperament and personality. Both men cared deeply for people, no matter who they were or how desperate their need. For four hours each morning from 8.00 am, Ross's house was 'like a public office' with church workers, members and 'poor people in distress' visiting him, with no one being turned away. The following details about Ross as a man and a minister are worth highlighting because they illustrate how much alike the two men were:

- Mr Ross cannot rest, and outside even his own congregation he is in 'labours oft'.
- There is never a frown seen on his face; he has a kind word for one and all and helps and gives to those in need.
- It is not unusual for him to leave his church at 10.00 pm and then visit the sick and dying of his flock until a late hour.
- His powers as a preacher are of a high order and his apt illustrations and speeches are attractive and memorable.

The similarities between Ross and Pugh in terms of character, kindness, motivation and unselfish commitment to people and the work of the gospel are striking and they found in each other quality fellowship and mutual understanding as well as support. Pugh learnt a great deal from the work being done in Cowcaddens and one example is in 1893 when he took his teenage daughter Annie[2] with him to Ross's church for their Convention. She explains the reason her father had:

He was eager for me to see the Sisters of the people working in and for the church … The Rev. William Ross spoke one day to a very poor lady about her soul but she looked sadly at him and replied, 'Oh Mr Ross, if you were as hungry as I am you would not have time to consider your soul.'

Moved by her words, Ross shared news of the incident with Lord Overton who offered to support six experienced Christian nurses to work

---

2 Her married name was Annie Pugh Williams.

Scotland and Wales

among the poor women in Cowcaddens; but, in addition, six Sisters of the people who had received training in the local Bible Institute worked among the prostitutes. Both the nurses and the Sisters lived among the people. Their work was effective in improving life for many in the area, with a steady stream of women being converted and joining the church as members. While in Cowcaddens, Annie describes how she dressed in a Sister's uniform for safety one night and accompanied one of the Sisters in her work. The teenager was afraid and ashamed at what she saw and heard, longing to love and help the young women.[3]

John Pugh himself was deeply moved by the work of these Christian nurses and Sisters of the people and determined to do something about similar social needs in the Cardiff area. An immediate step forward was the formation of 'The Women's Branch' of the Forward Movement a year later in 1894, largely through Mrs Pugh's initiative, with the immediate support of at least three hundred women. Following the example of the Cowcaddens church, Pugh planned to 'inaugurate a new order of (full time) women workers to be called "Sisters of the people"' to assist the evangelists in the growing Centres by caring for women in their varied, often desperate, needs and condition. Pugh wrote:

I am persuaded that a bird could as soon fly with one wing as the Church of God can evangelise the great centres of population without Christ-possessed women to go in and out among the suffering poor. There is a work no-one can do for Christ but them. It must be left for ever undone unless they turn to do it by providing the means or volunteering to do it themselves.[4]

It was not until 1903 that Pugh's plan was formally adopted by the General Assembly and only after one of Pugh's evangelists working in the notorious Saltmead area of Cardiff had shared bluntly in the Assembly what life was like for many women there:

---

3 *Atgofion am John Pugh*, pp. 37–38.
4 *The Romance of the Forward Movement*, p. 159.

Chapter 13

From three hundred to four hundred fallen women reside in my district. There are more than one hundred houses empty of families because they have been occupied for immoral purposes. I know girls going straight from sabbath school to the streets and thirty of them have gone since I am at Saltmead. These girls are expected to adopt this life even by some of their parents.[5]

Following this stirring speech, the General Assembly unanimously agreed to Pugh's plan and within four years there were eight Sisters working among vulnerable and needy women in Forward Movement Centres.[6] But Pugh was still not satisfied because a Home was urgently required for those enslaved in prostitution and who had become single mothers. Who would care for them? Help was near at hand. The Women's Branch was supportive of the project, and then in 1903 Mrs Tydfil Thomas of Cardiff agreed to organise this social aspect of the work; she has been described as 'a Welsh evangelical pioneer in social work'[7] and was a superb organiser and motivator. Largely as a result of the 1904–05 revival, some of these women prostitutes were being converted and attending churches, which challenged the more respectable church members to the need for a home. Early in 1905 Mrs Thomas wrote an article in the Movement's monthly paper, *The Torch*:

How pressing the need for a Home is … recently at a revival meeting in the centre of Cardiff, fifteen women were drawn by the cords of Christ's love to abandon their life of shame. They met together in one room. What shall we do with them? The Nonconformists in Cardiff have no home, no shelter to offer them. Accommodation was found for two in the Salvation Army Shelter while the other thirteen, precious souls for whom Christ died, had to retire to their old haunts.

---

5   *The Romance of the Forward Movement*, pp. 159–160.
6   The Sisters of the People were a huge help in the work of the Forward Movement undertaking social relief work, caring for women and assisting ministers. Over the decades their role changed significantly with the shortage of Ministers when some Sisters preached in churches and assumed responsibility for a Forward Movement Centre. The first woman ordained to the Christian Ministry by the Presbyterian Church of Wales was in 1978.
7   *Grace, Grit & Gumption*, p. 104.

Scotland and Wales

A gift was received from North Wales enabling the purchase of a House in Grangetown which was opened in November 1905 and named 'Treborth'. The House functioned effectively as a shelter and home for these women, then a larger house in Canton was opened two years later. The success of this venture in caring for younger women was widely respected and even commended in Parliament.[8]

Our interest is in the link between John Pugh and William Ross, for his visits to Glasgow confirmed the need to help people socially and practically in the context of gospel outreach. Other Forward Movement evangelists also preached and helped in the work in Cowcaddens: Seth Joshua was one of these evangelists. Recovering from illness, Seth delayed his trip to Glasgow for a few days and left on Tuesday 19th January 1904 but found the journey 'long and tiring'. Although feeling weak on arrival, Seth 'was refreshed with the news that the work had prospered at Cowcaddens'. He stayed in Glasgow until 3rd February and over one hundred people had trusted in Christ during the time he was there. On his return journey to Cardiff he was accompanied by William Ross whose purpose was to have treatment in Cardiff at Houghton's Hydropathic Home, but he attended numerous meetings and spoke often over the following weeks. Almost immediately on 6th February the two men spoke in the Police Institute in the central Cardiff, with Seth remarking:

Mr Ross also took part with much grace and dignity. How rich and ripe is the experience of my friends. His voice is not the voice of a novice on any subject. It is a pleasure to sit at his feet.[9]

Ross was speaking again, for example, at the opening of the forty-fourth Hall at Moorsland Road, Cardiff. While Ross had visited Wales many times and supported the work of the Forward Movement, this was his last visit. In his diary for 23rd April, 1904, Seth Joshua wrote:

---

8 *Atgofion am John Pugh*, pp. 61–62.
9 *Seth and Frank Joshua*, pp. 65–67.

Chapter 13

I heard on Newport platform that dear Mr Ross had passed away at Glasgow. I have lost a dear friend. He was the embodiment of kindness, and the most loving man I have ever seen, and hence the most Christlike I have ever known. Poor Cowcaddens church! There will be tears there tomorrow. Ross gave to those people his life-blood. Hundreds owe to him everything worth having. Dear brother, you were kind to me. May I emulate you and meet you in the better land.

Seth's loss and sadness was even more keenly felt by John Pugh who would also himself enter glory three years later due to exhaustion and overwork.

In 1899, in recognition of his work in Scotland but also his support for the Forward Movement in Wales, Ross had been invited to the Annual General Assembly to deliver several addresses which were well received and appreciated.

We now turn to consider the final years in the life of John Pugh.

14. The final decade

The final ten years of Pugh's life and ministry were marked by increasing tiredness as he continued to give himself to the work to which he felt so committed. He longed to develop the work further and there had been considerable success, so that by 1898, the first six years in the history of the Forward Movement, there were as many as thirty new churches established. At a Forward Movement meeting in Swansea in the Autumn of 1897 it was reported that the growth of the Forward Movement in those first six years had 'been instrumental in rescuing 15,000–20,000 men and women from the slums' and degradation. The Movement had also added significantly to the number of churches and buildings in the denomination. Principal Prys referred to an 'improvement' in that through the Forward Movement under Pugh's leadership and vision:

We are discovering afresh that the function of the church is not merely to educate and edify but also and primarily to evangelise. We earnestly hope that churches as a whole will respond to the note of advance Mr Pugh and his noble band have sounded...[1]

The 'improvement' referred to by Principal Prys in the work was, however, taking a heavy toll on John Pugh's health. Fielder is correct in claiming that 'the responsibilities he bore in the last decade of his ministry were colossal'.[2] There were endless requests for him to preach. Finance was needed to pay off the debt on the growing number of new Halls and church buildings. More evangelists were also required and those already working under the Movement needed caring for and encouraging.

---

1 *The Monthly Treasury*, Vol. 4, No. 47, November 1897, pp. 5–6.
2 *Grace, Grit & Gumption*, p. 99.

Chapter 14

South Africa

More people became concerned about Pugh's health and in 1896 Pugh and an ordained colleague from Pontypridd, William Lewis, were encouraged to visit the Welsh community in South Africa. The purpose was rest and relief for Pugh, but from that perspective the visit was a failure. Pugh was warmly welcomed by locals and immigrant Welsh people in all the towns they visited, with both men preaching regularly and more often in Welsh to the immigrants. Pugh's passion for preaching the gospel and seeking the conversion of unbelievers as well as their growth in Christ could not be confined to Wales or Scotland! During the visit, Pugh was 'shocked' by the spiritual needs of Welsh immigrants and the immoral conditions prevailing in the towns, especially Johannesburg. He longed to establish Forward Movement centres in these places and was disappointed that his denomination had made no provision for the Welsh people then living in South Africa. He reported:

We are persuaded more than ever, that as a church we shall do far more good among the British in South Africa by planting the Forward Movement flag there than by any other line of action.[3]

Being a man of action, on his return to Wales Pugh immediately called on his denomination to consider the desperate spiritual needs of Welsh-speaking people in South Africa. He wrote regular reports on this need and there was some support for him, including from the Rev. J. T. Lloyd, a native of Corwen in North Wales who was a leading Presbyterian minister in Johannesburg and who had suggested establishing an interdenominational Welsh church in the city to meet the need.

Rhyl was the location of the General Assembly when it met in May 1897, and the Committee considering the 'Welsh Dispersion' reported:

There were about 300 Welsh people in Capetown, and that the Rev. John Pugh, during a brief visit to that town in 1896 conducted a Welsh service in a church full of Welsh people, many of whom had not attended a place of worship for many years.

---

3 *Romance of the Forward Movement*, pp. 130–132.

More information was shared:

In Johannesburg there were at least 1,000 Welsh people, and that for their spiritual welfare Welsh services were held once a month with an average attendance of 150; and that these services were conducted by the four Welshmen who were members of English churches in this city.

In the Assembly proceedings, Pugh argued that one or two ministers should be sent to meet this spiritual need, using the Forward Movement as a pattern for developing the work there. A decision was made for a deputation of three men to be sent to South Africa to encourage the Welsh communities, and possibly afterwards to provide a minister from Wales to serve there. To Pugh's great disappointment, nothing happened and the subject was dropped. His holiday in South Africa had turned into a busy schedule of work, serving only to deepen his burden for reaching more and more people, wherever they were, with the gospel.

America

Pugh's visit as a delegate to the Pan-Presbyterian Alliance Congress in America in the summer of 1899 appears to have been more restful, though he made a deep impression on those present by his report of the work in Wales and he also taught them some of the new hymns being sung in Wales! It was during this visit that the University of Kentucky conferred on Pugh the honorary doctorate of Divinity in recognition of his work with the Forward Movement. On his return, the Forward Movement Directors recorded:

That this meeting expresses its good pleasure on the safe return of the Rev. John Pugh from his visit to the Pan-Presbyterian Alliance in Washington, and desire to thank God for His protection and for the success which attended his services there. Also it recognises with much pleasure the distinction and honour which the Central College, Kentucky, bestowed upon him, by conferring upon him its Diploma D.D, which was regarded as a direct recognition of his services connected with the Forward Movement.[4]

---

4 *Romance of the Forward Movement*, pp. 193–194.

Chapter 14

Following his visit to America, Pugh threw himself unreservedly once again into the work of the Forward Movement. There was an urgency attached to the work he did, an urgency driven by a longing for people to be saved. The responsibilities, however, were colossal with now over forty new churches established and other centres planned. He was in demand in terms of encouraging the evangelists, while there was a growing debt on the new buildings. Was he being reckless in initiating new centres and new churches when there was inadequate finance? That was what some critics claimed. There were also reports to prepare for committees and the editing of the monthly magazine. The burden was too heavy, especially as there was a constant demand for Pugh to preach in churches and lead missions in various places. Finally, after twelve years of leading the Movement alone, in 1903 some relief was provided with the appointment of the Rev. John Thomas as Pugh's assistant who would help with the vast amount of administrative responsibilities and general oversight of the work. This was an appropriate appointment as he had proved himself in Acrefair, Wrexham, as a good pastor, preacher, evangelist and administrator who would be missed in that area. Pugh also felt that he was 'a man after his own heart', possessing a similar zeal for the gospel. Part of his responsibilities in Cardiff would be to serve temporarily as the part-time evangelist in charge of the Heath Hall Church.

While relieved of some aspects of the work, Pugh remained as busy as ever during his final years. Among his many earlier engagements he had been preaching in early 1897 in the opening of the Hall at Malpas Road, Newport. An interesting insight into Pugh's situation is given by a pastor who called unexpectedly to see him in the late summer of 1898. He reported:

Fortunately, I found him at home and in excellent health and best of spirits. In less than five minutes we went to see the Grangetown Forward Movement Hall, a fine structure and well located … Mr Pugh confirmed he was about to remove to north-east Cardiff to start another Centre and the church at Grangetown has its eye on an able successor to carry on the work.[5]

---

5 *The Monthly Treasury*, Vol. 5, No. 57, September 1898, p. 19; see also p. 26.

The final decade

In the evening, the visitor accompanied John Pugh to the East Moors Hall to witness Mr Pugh baptising the daughter of the Rev. H. G. Howell

who continues to labour with marked success at this the first and pioneer centre of the Forward Movement.

At this time, Presbytery sanctioned the erection of a new Forward Movement Hall in Cathays, 'the sixth church established in the town under the Forward Movement'. There were difficulties obtaining the land, but through the means of a timely gift the 'Rev. John Pugh was enabled to secure the site'. Pugh's workload was varied, including buildings, sites for building, preaching, pastoral care and liaising with staff and committees. In the Autumn presbytery that year, we find that

the Rev. John Pugh had consented to assist Earlswood ... the most helpless of our churches.[6]

Ever willing to assist churches and to take the gospel to the unchurched, Pugh found it difficult to decline invitations or to close his eyes to the pressing needs of churches and communities. Two years later

the Rev. John Pugh, DD, reported that a new church had been incorporated at Barry Dock.[7]

Barry Dock

The background to this development is engaging and merits more attention.

Both the Romans and the Vikings had identified Barry as an ideal base for their raids and travels, while during the Middle Ages many pilgrims were attracted to the ancient St Baruc's church on Barry Island. Four visits to this church were deemed equivalent to one visit to Rome! A

---

6 *The Monthly Treasury*, Vol. 5, No. 59, November 1898, p. 24.
7 *The Monthly Treasury*, Vol. 1 (NS), No. 10, October 1900, p. 12.

Chapter 14

more dubious part of the history was the activity of many smugglers in the eighteenth century when Barry Island served as a key centre for their activities with one smuggler, Thomas Knight, having several armed smuggling ships operating in the Bristol Channel!

From the 1880s the huge potential of Barry was identified by industrialists for facilitating the growing coal industry in South Wales. There was also need to relieve the Tiger Dock area in Cardiff and increase coal exports from David Davies's Rhondda coal mines; so plans were made to develop Barry Docks with permission from Parliament. Work on Dock 1 started in November 1884 and opened in 1889, while Dock 2 was opened several years later. A railway was then required, so the Barry Railway Company was formed to carry coal from the collieries to Barry Docks, and by 1913 Barry became the largest coal export port in the world.[8] David Davies and his son Edward were the driving forces behind this development. Both men had contributed generously to Pugh's work and the son, Edward, had agreed to become the General Treasurer for the Forward Movement. Both men were interested in the welfare and spiritual needs of the people in these industrialised areas. Their sense of responsibility for the spiritual needs of local workers and families encouraged John Pugh with varying degrees of financial support and goodwill, but Pugh developed a closer relationship with Edward who died in 1898 as a relatively young man. Before he died, Edward told Pugh: 'Be sure you do something for Barry Dock.'

Pugh needed no reminder of the challenge to develop evangelism in Barry, but there were other pressures on his time and energy. Losing a close and reliable friend like Edward Davies was a huge blow to him. Other areas, too, demanded Pugh's attention, and then there was a small Christian mission already serving in the Docks area of Barry which had met with some success. This mission struggled financially, so early in 1900, two years after Edward's death, the Forward Movement assumed responsibility for mission work in the locality, and by 1902 a large hall seating seven hundred people with a smaller place attached was built at a cost of £4,000. Named as 'Dinam Hall' in recognition of the Llandinam

---

8 www.barry.cymru/history

The final decade

family's generosity to the work, the Hall was opened in April 1903 by David Davies who later became Lord Davies of Llandinam. An ordained medical missionary to India, Griffith Griffiths, was compelled due to ill-health to remain in Wales, and after serving as pastor of a Presbyterian church in Holywell, North Wales, he agreed to use his experience as pastor/evangelist—and medical doctor—as the evangelist serving the Barry Centre during the First World War period, which he did effectively.[9]

Christmas Day 1904, Seth Joshua's diary reads:

> 25 Dec (Sunday). I preached today at Barry Dock, but never did I have a harder day. It was against wind and tide all the day.

He then led a week's mission, so on New Year's Day (Sunday) 1905 he reports:

> I enjoyed a good day at Barry Dock and preached with freedom. In the evening service three people came boldly to the front. The prayer of one man when he found the light was touching…

For Monday 2 January, Seth Joshua wrote:

> Tonight I gave the story of my life at Barry Dock Hall. Dr Pugh and his brother, Edward, who had been converted at Crwys Hall on the Sunday night, came with me. He told me he had seen a vision of his family in heaven, all complete except himself; and his mother called him, saying, 'Come, Edward, we are all here except you.' This broke him down and he came out.[10]

John Pugh must have been greatly encouraged by his brother's conversion and to observe further blessing on the work in Barry Dock Hall. Perhaps his thoughts frequently returned to his deceased friend, Edward Davies, who had been such a support to him in the work with his

---

9 *Romance of the Forward Movement*, pp. 141–144.
10 *Seth and Frank Joshua*, pp. 80–81.

Chapter 14

concern for the spiritual needs of the population in the Barry Dock area. The work there was now well under way.

Memorial address[11]

A memorial service had been held for Edward Davies on 16th January, 1898, in the Park Hall, Cardiff, which held near to 3,000 people, and it was John Pugh who was asked to give the address. Despite having to restrain his emotions, Pugh was 'wonderfully helped' in delivering the address. Referring to his friend as 'an all-round prince', he described the ways in which Edward Davies had been a prince.

'First, he was *a prince in our world of commerce*', having inherited from his father the lucrative coalfields, and he had also been involved in Welsh railways and 'the great Barry Docks'. He was a steward of his riches 'and no shady transaction was acceptable' to him or to his Lord; 'he carried on all his vast concerns with clean hands and clean lips, for he was never known to take a mean advantage of anyone'. But, second, 'Mr Davies was *a prince in our education world*', continuing his father's deep interest and support for education in Wales, including the University College, Aberystwyth. 'Third, Mr Edward Davies was *a prince in our religious world*'. His parents were devoted Christians who had a profound influence on his life 'which was rooted and grounded in love' enabling him to 'overcome the temptations of wealth and … the torrents of iniquity … This too accounted for the deep interest he felt for the salvation of his fellow creatures at home and abroad'.

At this point, Pugh revealed something of his own heart and the depth of appreciation he had for the deceased Edward:

When the deplorable moral and spiritual condition of tens of thousands in Cardiff, and the great mining centres of Glamorgan and Monmouth was almost crushing me, and when God laid it on my heart … I poured out my heart to Mr Davies at the beginning of 1891 and told him all that was in it … he sent me a most kind letter asking what he could do for me. To which I replied—'Please act as a treasurer for the

---

11 An outline of this address is included in full in *Grace, Grit & Gumption*, pp. 209–211.

The final decade

enterprise.' This he consented to do, and that before there was a church or committee at my back. He was more than a friend to the Forward Movement, he was the brother born of God to back it up in every way. He never faltered—for he was a man of grit, grace and gumption ... a man with a grand moral backbone ... he gave thousands of people confidence in the Movement right away ...'

While Edward Davies attended the Movement's Committees and showed interest in the details of the work, Pugh goes on to explain that

the part that moved him to the depths and lit up his eyes like the midday sun, was to hear of sinners turning to God and submitting to Jesus Christ. This was clear evidence that he was more than a moral man, and that he was a regenerated and Christ-possessed man, for what moved the heart of Jesus moved him the greatest, and what moved heaven most, moved him the greatest; and we know what does that! It is not financial prosperity, it is not great victories on the battlefield or the triumph of a party at an election, but the conversion of a sinner to God ... The salvation of a soul makes God to sing, and gladdens the heart of the crucified but now enthroned Christ to overflowing ... until heaven's concentric ranks are one great sea of song and gladness. The conversion of sinners enhances the joys of earth and heaven.

John Pugh concluded his stirring appreciation of Edward Davies by issuing a personal challenge to Christians and church leaders:

... Who will serve the King? Who will step into this great breach which death has made in our princely ranks?

However, for Pugh there was 'another question which goes before that' and which is foundational to Christian discipleship and usefulness:

Who will surrender himself to Christ our saviour, and consecrate himself or herself to Christ our king? No one can fill this void unless he first commits himself to Christ and is possessed by His Spirit. The breach is too great for any Christ-less soul to fill. But with Him, every gap can be filled, every difficulty overcome and every good accomplished. For one who knew this by experience said: 'I can do all things through

Chapter 14

Christ who strengthens me'—I can live right; I can do right; I can suffer; I can die! This is the one thing needful to make burning and shining lights … this is what our country needs…

Pugh ended with what was a prayerful request and longing overflowing from his burdened heart:

May God who made such a Christian man of Mr Edward Davies, make many more who, like him, shall adorn the doctrine of Christ our Saviour in all things, and become a blessing to their race and a glory to the gospel which he believed and practised. Amen.

Huge loss

In the final decade of Pugh's life, the death of this close friend was the biggest and saddest loss and disappointment he experienced. Regarding his personal support for Pugh and also the Forward Movement Pugh had initiated, Edward Davies was loyal, generous and wholehearted out of love for Christ to see the work prosper. He was an outstanding supporter of this Movement and used his wealth and influence in many ways in order to express support.

For so many reasons Pugh had valued Edward's support and fellowship. A married man with three children, Edward attended a Welsh-speaking Presbyterian church, for he was a fluent Welsh language speaker. During the 1880s, there were very few English-language Presbyterian churches, but Edward quickly recognised that the majority of people moving into the new industrial areas of Wales did not understand Welsh and he recognised the rightness of Pugh's desire to provide English-language preaching and church services for them. Edward did not need any convincing, for he saw this urgent need. Furthermore, Pugh had many critics, some of whom were eager to preserve, even promote, Welsh language services and churches, despite the crying need for English language churches. Others felt Pugh was being too impetuous and ambitious in majoring on evangelism in these industrial areas of Wales. Many of the critics contacted Davies personally or wrote to him expressing their grievances concerning Pugh's

The final decade

work and plans. The fact that finance was required and that debts on the new buildings were increasing made Pugh an easy target for criticism. Nevertheless Edward Davies fielded these criticisms well, always reaffirming his unqualified support for the Forward Movement and Pugh himself. He also argued, in the light of Home Office reports highlighting the existence of drunkenness, immorality and violence in South Wales, that the Forward Movement was leading the way in addressing these social needs and poverty. The gospel would effect profound changes in society when people trusted in Christ and became new persons in Him.

Like Pugh, Edward Davies believed firmly that people everywhere needed to hear and respond to the glorious love of God in Christ. When he died at the age of forty-five in 1898, Pugh suffered a huge loss and one wonders to what extent this contributed to his burdens and loneliness during his final years. He had lost a valuable, trusted friend with whom he was able to share and open his heart to.

On the other hand, Pugh was not without his supporters, including influential men like College Principals. One of the three principals[12] who supported him was Owen Prys who served as president of the Forward Movement for forty years. An outstanding academic, a stirring preacher and a man who lamented the lack of preaching Christ crucified in the churches, his practical support for Pugh and his work was important. He also appreciated the work of the evangelists in the various Centres, even though they had not been formally trained in the denomination's Colleges in Trefeca or Bala.

It is now time for us in the next chapter to outline the closing months of Pugh's life.

---

12 D. Charles Davies, T. Charles Edwards and Owen Prys.

15. The closing months

There was a disturbing item of news concerning John Pugh in the August 1901 edition of *The Monthly Treasury*, news which must have caused concern throughout the Forward Movement and other churches. The news item was terse but supportive:

We regret to hear of the illness of the Rev. John Pugh, DD, Cardiff. The incessant burden of his great work is wearing him down and, although he has been gifted with a very powerful physique, yet such a complex responsibility as that of the Forward Movement has been more than even he could stand. We hope he will take at once the complete rest which he needs.

Two years earlier he had travelled to the United States as a delegate to the Presbyterian Congress but also for 'a real holiday'. Although feeling refreshed returning home, the stress and busyness of the work contributed to an increasing degree of physical weakness. Over the years Pugh had failed to ensure regular meals for himself or ensure an adequate sleep pattern. Throughout 1904 he had overworked despite his tiredness. We are not informed of the details of his illness in late 1905 except that he rested for several weeks. Pugh never found it easy to rest or withdraw from the work as he was always eager to preach, counsel and oversee the growing work. It is no surprise to read that on failing to attend a Directors' meeting of the Forward Movement in December 1905, further concern was expressed concerning his health:

The Directors expressed sorrow at seeing the absence of Dr John Pugh and at hearing the state of his health. They sincerely trust and pray that he may have a speedy recovery and urge him to take immediate rest; and that, in his absence, Revs Lewis Ellis and John Thomas be empowered to carry on the work.[1]

---

1   *Romance of the Forward Movement*, pp. 197–201.

The closing months

The Directors advised him to take a holiday overseas and visit the Holy Land with his wife which he agreed to do. The plan was to include a visit to Egypt, but the trip was plagued by problems such as bad weather in the Mediterranean, then fierce weather conditions prevented the ship docking in Alexandria which was then redirected to Beirut. A train journey to Damascus was then necessary but a snowstorm and Pugh's deteriorating chest condition alarmed his wife who persuaded him to return home rather than proceed to Jerusalem as planned. The decision was providential as her husband needed urgent medical attention and rest. Their unexpected early return to Wales meant that Pugh could attend the stone-laying ceremony for the new Heath Church building in Cardiff on 4th April 1906. People in attendance there noticed his weakness though he remained his own joyful self in their company.

A few weeks later Pugh was in Liverpool for the General Assembly and supported on the Assembly floor a motion that a committee should be appointed to ascertain as accurately as possible the number of non-churchgoers in Wales and suggest ways of responding to the challenge. Pugh was appointed secretary of the committee due to his organising abilities.[2]

He now preached less frequently, but in late September 1906 the Memorial Hall in Cardiff was opened with John Pugh as the preacher and his message was greatly appreciated. He remained busy despite deteriorating health, although his wife, Mary, fulfilled some engagements on his behalf. Family, friends and the Forward Movement leaders all urged him to rest more, which he found difficult to do.

Debt

One of the burdens Pugh felt more deeply at this time was the increasing debt incurred in purchasing sites and building halls/churches. The lack of finance also restricted the extension of the work as Pugh would have liked. There were a few Christian businessmen who contributed generously but more money was needed. A number of major disappointments made him

---

[2] *The Monthly Treasury*, Vol. 11, No. 5, May 1906, p. 7.

Chapter 15

even more concerned about finance. Edward Davies's death in 1898 had represented a major loss in terms of personal fellowship he had enjoyed with this generous businessman. Davies had also served as treasurer for the Movement and in that capacity had influenced others to contribute towards the work. Another generous donor, Richard Davies, had died in 1905, followed soon after by the death of the well-known Rev. David Lloyd Jones, a popular preacher who had influenced others to support Pugh's work.

There had been another disappointment for Pugh. In August 1899 *The Torch*, which had become the Forward Movement's monthly paper, announced the creation of 'The Twentieth Century Fund' and included the message:

Let us pray for the protection and guidance of the Lord during the century which is about to begin … This fund is for the immediate relief of places where we have lost and are losing ground at home. It is a rescue work, first and foremost.

The October 1899 Issue of *The Monthly Treasury* referred to this as a Centenary Fund intended as a Thanksgiving Fund to raise £100,000

for the purpose of pushing forward our work more effectively in the future … The history of the Forward Movement is a very bright one … We are trying to do … the work which Howel Harris would have undertaken had he been here …

The General Assembly had positively sanctioned the launch of this Centenary Fund and all the churches were urged to contribute in order to obtain the handsome sum of £100,000. A further appeal for contributions as a 'special act of gratitude' was made in the March edition of *The Monthly Treasury*. The outcome of the Fund was that the Forward Movement received only £15,000 to repay the debts on new buildings which, though a help, still left a large debt to repay. Historians may have failed to recognise the burden and disappointments Pugh experienced when faced daily with the challenge of finance and repaying debts. The question of finance had cast its dark shadow over him, especially during his final months.

The closing months

At midnight on New Year's Eve, Annie Pugh Williams describes her father sitting at his study desk writing letters of appeal to people he thought could support the work financially. The family were not allowed to disturb him because these letters were late in going out and needed to be sent as soon as possible. Her father occasionally stopped writing with his head leaning over the desk. He was overcome with tiredness which made letter-writing extremely difficult for him. She quotes her father saying to her on this occasion:

'Everyone thinks', he said, 'I enjoy asking for money, because I am always doing so. God knows how contrary it is to my nature, and I hate it more each day, especially when I am forced to write confidential letters to people.'

The amounts of money he wanted were described by her father as being 'small' or 'trivial' compared to what was spent by people on themselves or given to their churches.[3]

Contrary to orders from his medical doctor, Pugh insisted on honouring a preaching engagement in Acrefair, Wrexham in North Wales. Although a tiring journey lay ahead of him in addition to the demands of preaching, he was determined to go. This was his last Sunday preaching engagement on 18th November 1906 and he was enabled to preach three times 'with great power' on that Sunday to a crowded Acrefair church. His final sermon opened up 2 Corinthians 13:5: 'Examine yourselves whether you are in the faith. Prove your own faith.' His subject was 'Proofs of Conversion' when he listed six evidences of conversion:

1) the surrender of the will to Christ,
2) a consciousness that our sins which are many are forgiven,
3) a taste for the Word of God,
4) a delight in speaking to God,
5) a desire for the salvation of others, and
6) a desire to be like Jesus Christ.

---

3   *Atgofion am John Pugh*, p. 50.

Chapter 15

Gospel advance

In the month he died, March 1907, an article written by Pugh appeared in the Forward Movement's magazine, *The Torch*. His long-standing vision and determination to advance the gospel, coupled with an earnest appeal for Christians to be involved, characterise the article:

We won't go back: Prince Henry of Netherlands pluck, no doubt, encouraged the lifeboat men on the Hook of Holland in their heroic attempts to rescue the perishing on board the ill-fated 'Berlin'. 'We won't go back to the Hague', said the Prince, 'before we save them, we must get them somehow.' And they saved fifteen. The Prince of Peace is with us in our attempt to rescue perishing humanity. 'He shall not fail nor be discouraged until he have set judgement in the earth.' Must we go back? The cry from Liverpool, London, Bristol and from two dozen densely populated areas in Glamorganshire and Monmouthsire for the help of the Forward Movement, is heart-rending to those who know their moral and spiritual needs. Are we to retreat owing to the lack of funds? Some of the most talented and Spirit-filled ministers have joined our ranks recently. We need more. With loyal support and the cheer of God's people we won't go back.

Happy in the Lord

How did John Pugh cope in his personal relationship with the Lord during this extended period of weakness and illness? His diary entry for early January 1907 provides the answer:

Sunday, January 6: I am very ill and confined to my bedroom. Perfectly happy in the Lord...

The statement is pregnant with significance for it describes the spirituality of the man. He loved the Lord and had always delighted in fellowship with his Saviour over the years. His prayer life had been central in his ministry and now that same intimate relationship with Christ was evident despite the frustrations and burdens he felt concerning the work. He appears to have been resting more in the Lord and accepting that in divine providence his work was almost over. The concerns for the work were expressed in prayer and in conversations with others. On 24th

The closing months

March, for example, before he died, the Rev. F. C. Cole visited and prayed with him. After the time of prayer, his daughter records his father saying:

Francis, will you accept the pastoral care of Heath Hall? They are without a minister and there is a great opportunity for God's kingdom there.

The Rev. Cole, who had recently experienced remarkable blessing and church growth in Tonypandy in the Rhondda Valley, agreed, and his ministry in Heath would also witness church growth under his pastoral care.

Later Dr J. Cunningham Bowie, Pugh's medical doctor, called to see the patient. They were close friends and Dr Bowie told Pugh's daughter, Annie, in the presence of his patient that

There is no need for your father to die: with his strong constitution he could live for another twenty years but he has burnt himself out. If the denomination had given him a telephone and a car and only the essential work to do ... he could have lived ...

Certainly a car and a telephone would have been an immense help to Pugh in developing the Forward Movement. However, the major problem was Pugh himself in failing to take adequate care of himself, especially since launching the Forward Movement. He listened graciously to advice given him and occasionally acted upon it in terms of taking a holiday. Nevertheless, his work schedule was far too demanding and intense due to his own burden for the advancement of God's kingdom. The unceasing demands made on his time in the rapid growth of what was a remarkable work of grace made it difficult for a man of such vision and compassion to rest adequately.

John Pugh took hold of his daughter's hand after Dr Bowie had spoken and remarked:

But the Saviour died when he was 33 and I am 60. Don't rust out but rather wear yourself out for His sake, my child.[4]

---

4 *Atgofion am John Pugh*, p.63.

Chapter 15

Later that day, Palm Sunday, 24 March, 1907, Pugh died and entered upon the glories of heaven.

Many lamented his death and his funeral was one of the largest witnessed in Cardiff. Many people throughout Wales and beyond knew of John Pugh and his work. He was greatly admired and loved. The funeral service was held in Crwys Hall which was crowded for the occasion and tributes were given to this Christ-loving evangelist who loved people so deeply, whatever their social status and needs.

For Pugh's daughter Annie, 'the real funeral service'[5] was held in Cathays cemetery. Near the grave there was spontaneous singing of hymns and then, before the committal started, one of the stalwarts and characters of Saltmead Hall, Jack Turner, shared freely the burden of Pugh's message:

Brothers, the one thing that John Pugh loved us to do above all else was to present ourselves to Christ. If we haven't done that already, let's do it now, and afresh, and utterly, as he taught us to do, so that we may be worthy to stand at the graveside. Now, my brothers, as for being able to live a worthy life in our own strength—a life similar to his—that we cannot do. But in Christ we are able to respond to his promptings in our hearts. May this day be a starting point in our lives and the start of a better life.[6]

The crowds of people present spontaneously shouted out 'Amen'. Hundreds stood alongside the path leading to the grave, especially many of the poor but believing members from various Forward Movement Centres who had travelled a distance to be present. They had benefited enormously from Pugh's ministry and were present to express their love and appreciation of his ministry. During the committal when the coffin was lowered into the grave, the Rev. John Williams spoke movingly, including the words:

When the flowers on the grave have all died and the gravestone will eventually be broken in the dust, John Pugh's work will continue to bear fruit.

---

5 *Atgofion am John Pugh*, pp. 67–68.
6 *Atgofion am John Pugh*, p. 68.

The closing months

The Rev. Morris Morgan, Swansea then prayed, and by the end many of the people were in tears as Seth Joshua announced the closing hymn.

John Pugh left £395 to his family, an amount which even at that time would have made him a 'comparatively poor man'. His legacy, however, to the church and the kingdom of God was an exceedingly rich one. One of the many Memorial Services for John Pugh was held in Briton Ferry Quarterly Association where they affirmed unanimously:

Dr Pugh was God's gift to the denomination. He was blessed far beyond his brethren, and led the denomination to a new field of labour, which had already yielded much fruit in saving souls from death. He created a new epoch in the history of the denomination and the religious life of the nation.[7]

And what a legacy! Within sixteen years, Pugh had been used of the Lord to start between 47 and 50 new Centres/churches which had over 6,000 members maintaining an active witness to Christ in their localities.

In the closing chapters we will look more closely at the man and his important priorities as Christ's servant.

---

7 *Romance of the Forward Movement*, pp. 200–201.

16. John Pugh and his critics

Although a godly man who sought the glory of God and the advancement of His kingdom sacrificially, Pugh was by no means perfect. Some of his failings have been referred to but John Pugh had many critics, even within the Presbyterian Church of Wales which he loved and valued.

One criticism was his impatience, for it appeared to others he was unable to wait for committees and Associations to respond to his appeals for assistance. On the other hand, if he had done so this could have meant waiting a very long time and getting little done. Was he impulsive by nature? Possibly, but he was a man of action, and once recognising a need he felt obliged to act quickly.

One serious criticism was that he did not consult others before taking action. That was clearly an impression some gained due to the speed at which Pugh developed the Forward Movement. The rapid growth and blessing on the evangelistic efforts undertaken by Pugh and his evangelists was remarkable and breathtaking. However, his critics were not aware of all the facts relating to Pugh's desire and willingness to consult with others. He may well have needed to consult even more than he did, but with whom? Who shared his vision and was able to give wise counsel? Apart from the Christian businessmen he often shared with and consulted, like Edward Davies, he consulted others whenever possible.

One interesting example relates to the Rev. Dr David Saunders (1831–1892) who had exercised powerful ministries in churches in Penclawdd, Aberdare, Liverpool, Abercarn and Swansea. In the latter town his ministry continued for twenty years until his death in 1892. He was an excellent preacher and greatly admired within the denomination for his gifts. His own life and that of the family were dogged by ill-health with three of his children dying during his Abercarn and Swansea pastorates. A question arises at this point. Before launching his mission in the Swansea area, did John Pugh consult this famous preacher? Some were doubtful, but the facts are clear. Saunders himself was not opposed to mission, as some suggested, and Pugh added:

I know of no one who had a deeper sympathy with evangelistic efforts ... I naturally consulted him before launching the Cardiff Evangelistic Movement...

Saunders's reply to Pugh was encouraging:

... now is the right time to make active efforts to win many souls for Christ in Cardiff ... This would be the best possible form of revival in religion which we stand in so much need of throughout the Principality.[1]

Many other examples can be provided where Pugh shared with colleagues and friends the vision he had. When he was concerned to encourage and increase the number of English language Presbyterian churches in anglicised industrialised areas, Pugh first shared his concern with friends, then soon afterwards initiated a meeting with four ministers and as many as nine laymen in his Pontypridd church and together they planned the first Conference for English-speaking churches which met in Swansea in 1884 and then annually thereafter. He was not a loner at all.

Similarly, Pugh's burden for a Training Home where students and trainees could stay while gaining experience in evangelism in Cardiff was discussed with others. Principal Davies, Trefeca, and also later Principal Prys, agreed such a House and practical training were urgently needed. They supported the project financially as they recognised the need to remove the 'missing link' between academic training in the Colleges and the more practical, pastoral work needed in churches but exemplified by the Forward Movement.

---

1 *The Christian Standard*, Vol. 2, No. 16, November 1892, pp. 8–9.

Chapter 16

Was he in too much of a hurry in establishing Centres for evangelism? Two of several examples can be provided which indicate that too often Pugh was restrained from moving forward. His close friend, Edward Davies, before his death in 1898 had remarked to Pugh:

Be sure you do something for Barry Dock.

There was early involvement in the Barry Dock area by another small mission which was eventually taken over by the Forward Movement in 1900. That work was not rushed in any way by Pugh. Or consider Principal Prys's appeal to John Pugh to do something for Merthyr. A few years elapsed before he was able to commence work in Merthyr, but that was not due to inactivity or lack of desire on Pugh's part:

Merthyr was constantly on Pugh's heart, but every suggested way appeared closed.

His response was to pray more specifically, asking the Lord to open the door for the gospel. This prayer was answered in March 2005 when a three-week mission led by Seth Joshua was held there.

Certainly the rate at which these Centres/churches were planted is astonishing, and yet at the same time there were many indications of divine restraint as well as blessing in this major outreach in industrial areas.

However, should this work of opening new Centres have been approached more cautiously? Sometimes a brake was imposed on Pugh, and one example is when the Glamorgan and Monmouthshire Presbytery.

reported that the church at Cowbridge Road (Cardiff), can undertake responsibility for a Forward Movement Centre at Pontcanna ... and the Secretary was instructed to write to the Rev. John Pugh, requesting him to take no definite steps until the brethren are assured of what is likely to be the requirement of the locality ...[2]

---

2 *The Monthly Treasury*, Vol. 2, No. 28, April 1896, pp. 23–25.

John Pugh and his critics

There was no opposition to his plan for a new work but a brake was applied wisely until others locally and in Presbytery were reassured concerning the genuine need of a Centre in that locality. And that is what happened; but often in the early period Pugh was pressing ahead, burdened with the desperate need to cater spiritually for the thousands of people in industrial areas. The need was too great to ignore or delay.

Often when arguing his case in denominational committees or Associations for support in evangelising the crowded industrial areas, his arguments were frequently accompanied by his tears over their spiritual plight. Was this a weakness? Not necessarily. His arguments for action in evangelising were strong and well-made as well as biblical, but Pugh's heart was profoundly moved by the plight of people without Christ. Even in acknowledging the force of his arguments, what often moved some doubters and critics were his sincerity, love and the depth of concern he felt for people who were socially needy and deprived of gospel witness.

Pugh was criticised too because he incurred significant debt on many of the new Centres/church buildings he built. Pugh felt this burden of debt and often urged people to contribute financially. He also trusted God as well as the denomination to meet the need. However, with the slow, disappointing financial support from churches and the deaths of several significant donors, ought Pugh to have been more responsible in this respect? Possibly the critics were right in this. On the other hand, the Forward Movement was now officially the responsibility of the denomination and should have been supported far better by it.

Close friends and co-workers were also concerned for the health of their leader. Blessed with a strong constitution, Pugh had a busy programme of work. His commitments were many and his zeal generated more work for himself. One result of this overworking was that he continued to miss regular meals, failed to obtain adequate sleep and rarely relaxed away from work. His one 'bosom friend' was William Ross in Glasgow, but he needed close friends near at hand to counsel, encourage and restrain him on occasions from the excessively long hours of work and constant travel to which he had committed himself. Hours before his death, Pugh's medical doctor remarked he could have lived longer if the denomination

Chapter 16

had given him more relief and support in the work, even a car and a telephone! Pugh had his faults and should have been more responsible with regard to his own health, but on the other hand the denomination should have been more supportive and caring for a man who was visionary, a 'pioneer', and whose work was blessed so remarkably in evangelism and church planting.

'Many golden qualities'

A few years following Pugh's death, Seth Joshua was asked why no biography of John Pugh had been written. Seth felt ill-equipped to answer the question and suggested it was a matter for the Presbyterian Church of Wales to decide. He added that if the question was shouted loud and clear throughout the valleys of South Wales, the mountains would respond with surprise as to why a biography had not appeared, for Pugh's impact and influence in these industrial areas had been extensive and profound. Many people owed their changed lives to the preaching of Pugh as well as his work in providing evangelists in their localities. He was greatly loved and respected. Seth was then asked whether he could suggest someone who would be suitable for writing Pugh's biography. His answer is worth repeating:

> Someone with a blind eye to his few failures and an open one to his many golden qualities. A writer in touch with his ideals and in sympathy with his ambitions. One who could hide himself, and reveal the subject of his biography.[3]

Interestingly, Seth refers to 'his few failures', but only in the light of his 'many golden qualities'. This balance is required, for Pugh was so very different. He stood out as a leader with a genuine heart love for people. He was a 'pioneer' of major significance. The testimony of Seth Joshua in this respect is powerful as he had worked closely with Pugh for several years and latterly had served as his second-in-command. Seth knew the man remarkably well.

---

3 *Seth and Frank Joshua*, pp. 112–113.

John Pugh and his critics

Following Pugh's death, 'An Old Friend' used a definition of 'genius' which included the statement, 'an eye to see, a heart to feel and an arm to carry out'.[4] He continued:

To my mind, Dr Pugh was one of the pioneers whom God has from time to time been giving to our Connexion ... he was a brave pioneer, a genius ...

What evidence did he have for this claim? Was he exaggerating? The case is argued well:

He had vision ... he saw the great need of his country and saw the great opportunity of his Connexion. He saw the rapid rush of people into the industrial areas of South Wales; he saw the inadequate provision religiously of Cardiff, Newport and Swansea ... he saw the diminishing charm of the chapel and ... saw the thousands who cared for neither God nor church, neither Sabbath nor Scripture; he saw the need, the tremendously urgent need of this land and saw the means of meeting it. Many others saw the need but did not see the remedy. He saw both ... and saw what the Connexion had not seen and led it to see the problem and the solution. He was eyes to his church. Was he not a pioneer?

Those words are pregnant with significance, hiding some of the significant, even overwhelming, tensions and challenges which Pugh had faced within his denomination. If Pugh 'was eyes to his church' in a changing situation, the denomination had a responsibility to care for him by providing greater financial and prayerful support for such a leader. There were tensions and challenges of which Pugh may not have adequately been aware.

What were these tensions and challenges? This question will be addressed in the next chapter.

---

4 *The Monthly Treasury*, Vol. 11, No. 5, May 1907, pp. 5–6.

17. Tensions and challenges

One can appreciate the ministry of John Pugh even more by becoming aware of some of the tensions and challenges he faced in reaching out to unchurched people in the industrial areas of Wales. In this chapter reference will be made to a few of these major challenges and tensions confronting the pioneer evangelist.

First of all, there was the relocation of many people for purposes of work from urban areas across Britain to the newly-developing industrial areas of South Wales, resulting in extensive social changes and needs. Church leaders were aware of this development but did little about it and were unsure how to respond. For Pugh himself, this was a huge challenge, one in which he needed to take action urgently.

Secondly, there was the inadequate provision of English language churches in these new industrial areas as centres for evangelism and the spiritual nurturing of converts. The Presbyterian Church of Wales in this period consisted mostly of Welsh language churches and conducted all its affairs in Welsh for there was only a small number of English language churches. Although bilingual himself, Pugh felt the desperate need for English language churches in industrial areas where the majority of people only spoke English.[1] This was a gospel, rather than a language, issue at heart for Pugh. To add to the seriousness of the situation, information was shared that 'the Roman Catholics have just inaugurated a forward movement for the conversion of the Welsh people'.[2]

---

1 To meet this need, as noted earlier, Pugh took the initiative in proposing and arranging the first English Churches Conference in 1884 at Swansea.
2 *The Christian Standard*, Vol. 2, No. 17, December 1892, p. 10.

Tensions and challenges

Thirdly, culturally and socially there was the diminishing appeal of the chapel in Wales coupled with growing ignorance of the gospel. For example:

A very serious decrease in Sunday School attendance was reported in 1901 and attributed to the popularity of sport, gambling, alcohol, secularising of the Sabbath and the loss of parental support. This decline was also reported in England and Scotland.[3]

The impact of these social changes in Wales resulted in

the separation of the people from the churches becoming wider and deeper.[4]

The variable spiritual condition of churches resulted too often in dwindling numbers attending church services, with church growth becoming more of a rarity.

Fourthly, the challenge for Pugh was deeper and possibly more complex than even he appreciated with regard to his own denomination. For example, a growing nominalism had developed within local churches accompanied often by a middle-class respectability. There were, of course, many lovely and dedicated members within the churches, like James Wilson (1834–1891) of Walton, Liverpool who had been converted in 1879 whose

rapid growth in grace and in the knowledge of Christ ... was simply marvellous ... The Spirit was working unimpeded in him.[5]

Early in 1891

when deeply concerned for the church he was distressed over the selfishness of Christians and their hardness, and that in Welsh Calvinistic Methodist churches.

---

3 *The Monthly Treasury*, Vol. 2, No. 1, January 1901, pp. 15–16.
4 *The Christian Standard*, Vol. 1, No. 9, March 1892, p. 2.
5 *The Christian Standard*, Vol. 1, No. 8, February 1892, pp. 6–7.

Chapter 17

In the same month, *The Christian Standard* referred to the history of the Calvinistic Methodists in Wales 150 years previously when the

revival began among the lower strata of society and worked its way up until it took hold of the middle class ... Now we are in danger of becoming respectable. Not long ago, a very large number of our deacons were labourers ... men of fervent piety and some strength of character ... The modern deacon is much more intelligent ... but perhaps less spiritual ... We are in danger of attaching too much importance to wealth and position in the election of deacons ... It is not long since some of the finest men of prayer in every church used to be labourers—men that could wrestle with God, whose prayers thrilled the congregations and brought heaven down to earth ... But such are becoming rare in the land.

This was echoed in different ways by others:

'Oh, the thousands in our Welsh churches who are doing nothing ...' is another report,[6] 'others, thinking as John Pugh put it the other day, that all spiritual work should be done by proxy ...'

Principal Prys had also warned in the Autumn of 1897[7] that when the church loses its first love of Christ then

it becomes contracted, leaving the masses out in its interest for the middle classes. It became an eminently middle-class institution ...

Nine years after the start of the Forward Movement, an article entitled 'The Outlook' was published which painted a penetrating and realistic picture of the condition of a significant number of local Presbyterian churches in Wales. Some had made no effort to reach the unchurched masses of 'strangers' who had 'inundated' the country while

---

6 *The Christian Standard*, Vol. 1, No. 10, April 1892, pp. 3–4.
7 *The Monthly Treasury*, Vol. 4, No. 47, November 1897, p. 4.

in other parts of the Principality the Connexion has allowed many of our congregations to dwindle so that we are now—as compared with the population of those places, actually weaker than we were half-a-century ago. We must not close our eyes to the fact we have many churches which have made no progress in the last fifty years, and others in a state of decay, dwindling in size, and assembling in almost half-empty buildings on the Lord's Day ... and struggled for 60–70 years ... is this due to a want of zeal and energy in pressing people to come to the Saviour ...?[8]

All was not healthy within Presbyterian Churches in Wales and the Border counties, despite the denomination having known periods of local, regional and national revival in its history.

Fifthly, there were further problems emerging during this period and one wonders to what extent Pugh had appreciated the 'wind of change' blowing gently at first through the corridors of the denominational colleges and the preaching of ministers. One important indicator was that Calvinism was in decline. In the Conference of English Churches in September 1901,[9] we are informed that

The meeting on Calvinism will linger long in the memory of all ... We were strengthened in our faith in Calvinism but if the vote was taken ... our denomination would cease to be officially registered as 'Calvinistic Methodist'.

The situation was indeed more serious regarding theology:

Many are astonished at references made both by questioners and witnesses to the teaching of Calvinism in the present Church Commission. The revelations are extremely disquieting. Is it that men do not know what Calvinism really is? Or is it they are afraid of confessing it or ceasing to believe it? We think they do not know what it is. A writer has recently said that the pest of Wales is its Calvinism. Evidently that poor man does not know what Calvinism is.[10]

---

8 *The Monthly Treasury*, Vol. 1 (NS), No. 2, February 1900, pp. 15–17.
9 *The Monthly Treasury*, Vol. 2 (NS), No. 11, November 1901, p. 6.
10 *The Monthly Treasury*, Vol. VIII, No. 7, July 1907, p. 18.

Chapter 17

An appeal was then made to the denomination for action regarding its 1823 Confession of Faith which was Calvinistic but under review at the time by a Commission:

In the present time it were well if the Connexion which essentially bears the Calvinistic name, could somehow put the Calvinistic teachings clearly before the people. The age needs them. It needs them profoundly. The tonic for this anaemic age is Calvinism. Against the wild imaginings of the New Theology, with its lowering of standards and its loosening of fibre, we need ... the masculine and ennobling statements of truth as set forth by Paul and Calvin. We commend to our authorities the desirability of some clear thinking.

Although written several months after his death, John Pugh would have been aware of the undermining of the denomination's subordinate Standard of Faith, namely, the 1823 Confession of Faith which ought to have been binding on all church leaders. Nevertheless, Pugh may not have recognised the extent to which the denomination was being freed from its biblical, Calvinistic moorings.

Sixthly, the wind of change had also affected preaching in the churches. Addressing students at Trefeca College in 1893, the Rev. J. Morris lamented that

Many ministers give themselves an almost unlimited latitude in the range of subjects which they preach about to the people—science, literature, art, philosophy and the political economy are not excluded from their homilies. Some do so for the sake of variety and freshness ... but a clear proof we have mistaken our profession. For example, Spurgeon was able to interest a great congregation of 5–6,000 people for approximately forty years yet limited to the cardinal ... truths of Christianity ... The pulpit has a special function and the Minister has a special task. He is not a jack of all trades. Some give themselves latitude because they have lost faith in the great doctrines of Christianity. When the minister is robbed of his proper themes, he is bound to find other themes ... to justify continuance of his office ... I pity the hungry sheep who look up but are not fed.

Tensions and challenges

This report on preaching in the 1890s in Wales is disturbing. For example, the reference to a 'range of subjects' outside the Bible forming the content of sermons and some preachers 'who have lost faith in the great doctrines of Christianity' points to a major decline in doctrinal, biblical preaching. The failure of a growing number of ministers to preach biblically with Christ crucified at the heart of their ministries was a major contributory factor leading to the serious decline of local churches. The response of the Rev. J. Morris is one which John Pugh would endorse enthusiastically:

What are the ruling ideas in Christian Ministry? The reply is the salvation of the soul ... and the gospel as the means of attaining that end...

Against this background, one can appreciate why Pugh was not usually invited to important preaching festivals in churches or Associations. He was concerned supremely to preach Christ crucified and in a way people could understand and relate to. We ought not to be surprised that many within the denomination were lukewarm in their support for Pugh's evangelistic ministry. Against this background, it is unsurprising that the financial support for Pugh's work was generally disappointing, and without the significant contributions of Christian businessmen Pugh's work would have suffered considerably.

Criticisms of Pugh need to be considered fairly in the light of his own beloved denomination which was moving slowly away from a God-centred gospel and consequently with little sympathy for the message so dear to Pugh's heart and a message which had been effective in saving many people in industrialised areas. Presbyterian churches were becoming more respectable, middle-class and uncertain concerning the foundational doctrines of the Christian faith. While Pugh was admired for pioneering evangelism in challenging industrialised areas, there was a half-hearted and muted response to his work from significant sections within his denomination.

Had he expected too much of his church leaders and local churches? I fear he did. He may not have recognised the depth of the cleavage

Chapter 17

within the denomination regarding loyalty to the Bible and the tenets of faith enshrined in their 1823 Confession of Faith. The dark clouds of unbelief were beginning to penetrate the denomination with the inevitable consequences of theological, spiritual and numerical weakness.

John Pugh was a pioneer greatly used of the Lord, but the army of churches he represented were mixed in their support and willingness to engage in essential gospel work with him. Sadly, these tensions and challenges continued with sad results for the churches and their communities.

What of John Pugh as the Lord's messenger? That is the question we will answer in the next chapter.

18. John Pugh: the Lord's messenger

What was John Pugh like as a preacher? Are there aspects of his ministry we can learn from? In this chapter we will consider him as a preacher in five related ways.

Following Pugh's death, Seth Joshua was asked his opinion of John Pugh as a preacher.[1] His answer was factual and started by saying that critics 'would answer this question by saying what he was not as a preacher'. Seth was familiar with what critics said about his colleague for he did not fit into the polished, respectable and learned style of preaching which had developed in Welsh pulpits where it was a type of preaching where the gospel of salvation was often assumed or even modified rather than declared biblically. Nor would Pugh entertain his hearers with the 'new ideas' which had become popular in churches. Consequently, Pugh was not regarded as a 'special' preacher who would be invited to preach on important church occasions.

Building on Seth Joshua's answer, there are five aspects of Pugh's preaching which stood out for his hearers, whether in the open air, in tents/centres or church buildings.

1. Christ-centred

Seth explained to his questioner that he could only give his opinion 'as to what Pugh was' as a preacher and what he had observed and listened to often over the years. Seth was better informed concerning Pugh's preaching gifts than any critic:

He often preached and wept at the same time, and his tears were as eloquent as words. His sermon glowed with a passion for souls ... He preached with one arm clinging

---
1 *Seth and Frank Joshua*, pp. 111–113.

Chapter 18

around the Cross, and with the other outstretched to snatch souls from the wrath to come.

While there are very few notes available relating to Pugh's preaching, all who heard him agreed that Jesus Christ crucified was at the heart of his preaching. Seth's description of Pugh preaching—'with one arm clinging around the Cross'—sums up well the centrality of Christ's death in his preaching. He had an overwhelming sense of indebtedness for God's love in Christ and the unique, substitutionary sacrifice of the Lord Jesus for sinners at Calvary. The wrath of God against sin and sinners was also prominent in his preaching in which he regularly warned hearers of the danger they were in if they died without trusting Christ. Seth Joshua added:

He found his way to Calvary from every text, or any part of God's word...

Principal Charles Edwards[2] addressed students in Trefeca College on the subject of preaching in June 1891. The great need of the Welsh pulpit, he insisted, was to avoid professionalism and to

believe the great fundamental truths, especially concerning Jesus Christ crucified and risen.

Pugh did that faithfully. One professor described the doctrine of the cross as

an instrument of many strings; while Christ crucified is the central point, it has a large circle of related truths

such as the Father's electing love, the sending of Christ into the world, the incarnation and its saving purpose, the Holy Spirit and His application of the benefits of redemption which is inseparably related to a life of

---

2 *The Christian Standard*, Vol. 1, No. 2, August 1891, p. 4.

usefulness and future glory.[3] Pugh was aware of this 'large circle of related truths' in proclaiming the Cross.

Concluding 'An Earnest Appeal for a Great United Action to Win Wales For Christ', Pugh made an appeal to believers:

Let us preach the same gospel and in the same spirit as Daniel Rowland, Howel Harris, Thomas Charles, John Elias, John Jones, Talsarn, Henry Rees and Owen Thomas did. Let us pray for an outpouring of the Divine Spirit.[4]

Pugh's daughter confirms that it was

a common view amongst ministers of the Presbyterian Church he belonged to that he was no preacher, although others who went to hear him thought otherwise ... When mother was asked what it was that she considered to be the greatest spiritual victory in my father's life, her answer was carefully weighed for she spoke from a close relationship with her husband and first-hand knowledge of his many struggles: 'He was willing to forgo being a preacher in the popular sense. He had the ability, the power and the intellect to be such, but he was willing not to be one, and to count himself as nothing, so that men did not hear him, but rather Christ.'[5]

Mrs Pugh's testimony is significant, revealing the deliberate choice her husband made with regard to the message he should preach. Rather than develop his gifts to become a much-sought after preacher in his denomination, he forfeited popularity and reputation in order to preach Christ and Him crucified. This was a choice reminiscent of the apostle Paul who also turned his back on personal reputation and popularity in order to glory in Christ as Saviour. The element of choice and sacrifice in preaching Christ is extremely important in considering Pugh's preaching, a preaching so powerfully used by God.

---

3 *The Christian Standard*, Vol. 2, No. 21, April 1893, pp. 2–3.
4 *The Christian Standard*, Vol. 1, No. 7, January 1891, pp. 9–11.
5 *Atgofion am John Pugh*, p. 45; *Grace, Grit & Gumption*, p. 167.

Chapter 18

2. Conversion

Many of the unchurched people Pugh and his evangelists preached to were often converted when they first heard the gospel preached or very soon afterwards. Pugh expected conversions, he preached for conversions and was disappointed if God had not been convicting sinners under the gospel and bringing them to trust Christ. Admittedly, he invited hearers after he had preached to show whether they wanted to respond to Christ, and they were counselled but not pressurised or coerced into making a 'decision'; but these unchurched people needed help in understanding what it meant to turn to God in repentance and trust in Christ. Nevertheless, a significant number of hearers, whether in the open air or in church services, were converted immediately, sometimes dramatically. The Lord still works in this way but that is not the norm. More often the Lord works through the means of grace over a period of time and this needs to be appreciated, otherwise we will be discouraged in gospel work.

Conversion to Christ is God's work which is rooted in, and evidence of, the miracle of regeneration when the Holy Spirit works supernaturally and inwardly in a person's life. That is what Pugh believed on the basis of the Bible and the denomination's 1823 Confession of Faith.

In this divine action, the individual is brought effectually to Christ and union with Him so that an intimate and spiritual union becomes the source and strength of the believer's life and fruitfulness. Only God can do this saving work and therefore one must use diligently and prayerfully those means God has promised to bless to bring people to the Saviour. That is why Pugh longed for others to hear the gospel because the Lord uses preaching and the hearing of the Word to bring people to Christ.

For the Rev. J. Morris, DD, a professor in Memorial College, Brecon, this

should be the great aim of the Christian minister to labour diligently and prayerfully for conversions. Then instruct them in the Word and holiness...[6]

---

6   *The Christian Standard*, Vol. 2, No. 21, April 1893, p. 2.

John Pugh: the Lord's messenger

It was appropriate that Pugh's last text which he preached[7] was 2 Corinthians 13:5: *'Examine yourselves whether you are in the faith. Prove your own faith.'*

His subject was 'Proofs of Conversion' when he listed six evidences of conversion. The verbs used by Pugh in describing the evidences of conversion underline its radical nature. Notice words like 'surrender', 'consciousness', 'taste', 'delight', and 'desire'. This was not an emotional, temporary 'decision' to follow Christ. By the Spirit's power, a sinner's will surrenders to Christ and is expressed practically in commitment to Christ, accompanied by new 'taste', 'desires' and 'delight' for the Lord, His Word and glory. Converts are new persons in Christ.

3. Compassion

Seth Joshua's description of Pugh's preaching with tears was no exaggeration:

... and his tears were as eloquent as words. His sermon glowed with a passion for souls ... He preached with one arm clinging around the Cross, and with the outstretched arm to snatch souls from the wrath to come.

Throughout his ministry the response of congregations was the same:

His fluency is increased by his earnestness; his appeals come from a heart burning with a desire to save souls ...[8]

Only a few weeks after Pugh's death, a friend captures the type of man he was:

John Pugh was not a man of brilliant intellect but a man of great heart.

Was he an emotional man who cried easily? Did he cry deliberately in an attempt to persuade hearers of his message? The answer to this question

---

7 Sunday 18th November 1906 in Acrefair, Wrexham.
8 *The Christian Standard*, Vol. 1, No. 2, August 1891, p. 2.

Chapter 18

is provided by an 'Old Friend' who wrote an Appreciation of Pugh after his death and remarked:

John Pugh had a heart to feel. Passion ... But this passion involving a true desire to bring his fellow people to Jesus Christ was one of the greatest gifts of Dr Pugh. In this ... he was above us all. His heart was sore at the sight of souls he saw. Teeming Cardiff—sheep without a shepherd, prodigals, careless, godless crowds—to him they were a daily heart burden. He yearned for their salvation ... critics thought he exaggerated ... But he was the heart to his church.[9]

The compassion he expressed resulted from his deep experience of the love and compassion of God in Christ. One writer who had observed Pugh over a long period testified that

he has a tender heart. He is to be seen at his best when praising his Saviour and when dealing with a troubled soul. There is in his heart a great sympathy for the fallen and troubled...[10]

4. Care

We need to view Pugh's pastoral care in the context of his denomination and the growing tendency to neglect the oversight of believers within the local church. An article appeared in *The Christian Standard* for March 1892 under the title of 'The Pastorate in the Presbyterian Church of Wales'. The main thrust of the article is that

effective pastoral work is the most essential element to the success of our churches ... but it seems the correct idea of pastoring is wanting...

The writer commends the pastoral care exercised in the early period of Calvinistic Methodism, for it was 'personal and thorough amongst the members'. Then a change occurred in that the

---
9   *The Monthly Treasury*, Vol. VII, No. 5, May 1907, pp. 5–6.
10 *The Monthly Treasury*, Vol. 4 (NS), No. 12, December 1903, pp. 12–13.

wave of powerful preaching on weekdays and Sundays swept over the country ... then came a lull in pastoral oversight for 50–60 years.

Although the importance of pastoral care was recognised thirty years previously in 1862, yet little was done by ministers to establish effective pastoral care. One reason is provided by this writer:

Pastors are carried away with the old idea of great preaching of one hundred years ago and think their great mission is to prepare splendid sermons for the Monthly Meetings (regional) ... at the expense of cultivating great pastoral ministry. Many say they must be in the study and prepare sermons but exclusively so. Why?

The writer then referred to the late Dr Edwards, Bala whose advice was:

If you want to enrich sermons and make them go direct to the human heart, leave your studies at times and visit the homes of the afflicted, listen to the experiences of the sick ... catch the whisperings of the dying—those are the things which will make you effective preachers.

He ended with a moving appeal:

Our young pastors ought to understand ... they must make it by their own pastoral success within their own churches and not simply by flying around with supposed crack sermons as in olden times. The churches are thirsting for real pastoral care...

In this respect Pugh was a model for other pastors. He mixed well with his people, visited them while he was a pastor and cared for individuals in the various centres he established under the Forward Movement.

Pugh emphasised the great need for love in ministry to people. Referring to the Lord's question to Peter in John 21 as to whether he loved Christ, and Peter's positive reply, Jesus said:

'Feed My lambs ... My sheep'—the one great qualification is LOVE ... All the learning and all the eloquence will not make you a successful soul witness unless your soul is

Chapter 18

all ablaze with love to Christ and with love for people. But the vilest may be rescued … the spirit of love.

In the early days of the Forward Movement, John Pugh underlined the same need of love:

Love is the great key … No one can be successful in God's work and in soul-winning unless they possess a passionate love for God and souls. This is our experience. O for more and more love for Jesus and people.[11]

5. Confidence

'Dr Pugh', we are informed, 'has two great qualities that keep him in the work—unlimited faith in God and almost unlimited faith in man …', the latter meaning he delegated work regularly to individuals he trusted.[12] The statement must not be misunderstood, for the writer explains:

Big schemes are natural to him and the courage with which he launches into them is the child of faith. He feels that the condition of things demands great plans, and he believes it is God's will that out of the riches of His glory, He will supply all that is necessary for their success.[13]

Pugh's confidence was in God and in His promises which was inseparably related to his diligence in personal prayer. His first open-air preaching meeting around the Town Clock in Tredegar in August 1872, referred to in Chapter 4, is recounted again here because it provides a fascinating insight into Pugh's praying. He was nervous and had asked for support from his church officers and members, but no one had responded when he was ready to start the service. Then six women from his church appeared

---

11 *The Christian Standard*, Vol. 1, No. 9, March 1892, p. 1.
12 Pugh believed that 'The secret of success in work is that you can place some of it on the shoulders of others'. One evangelist shared with deep appreciation the fact 'there was nothing so wonderful as the trust he had in us'. This provided space for his workers to develop their gifts and prove the Lord on a daily basis: *Atgofion am John Pugh*, p. 49.
13 *The Monthly Treasury*, Vol. 4 (NS), No. 12, December 1903, pp. 12–13.

and they stood alongside him; so, with the ladies singing the chorus of the hymn he began to sing: 'I hear Thy welcome voice'.

He needed God's help, so he prayed after the hymn and now reflected on that occasion:

> I had no idea how long I prayed, but when I opened my eyes after being on the Mount with God, a great crowd of men and women stood before me gazing in amazement into my eyes.[14]

Notice the phrase 'after being on the Mount with God'. Prayer was more than words for John Pugh. He was addressing the living, all-powerful and faithful God who had called and saved him. Pugh knew God, often wrestling in prayer with God in seeking His help and power in preaching the gospel. Pugh knew the approval of heaven, even if many of his ministerial colleagues had little respect for his preaching!

In the next chapter, we will begin to look at Pugh's empowering in his ministry by the Holy Spirit as he sought regularly to preach and glorify Christ.

---

14 *The Romance of the Forward Movement*, p. 17.

19. Word and Spirit (1)

In this chapter, we reflect on the extra-ordinary ministry which John Pugh exercised during the final decades of the nineteenth century until the commencement of the 1904-05 revival in Wales. By any standard, his preaching and that of his colleagues was remarkably effective, possibly knowing localised revivals.

To understand this preaching and its impact on so many lives and communities, we identify the following principles:

1. Pugh and his colleagues took seriously the Great Commission (Matthew 28:18–20; Mark 16:15)

The preaching of the Word and prayer are the means by which the Holy Spirit brings sinners to Christ and edifies believers. For that reason, the Lord commissioned His people to 'Go into all the world and preach the gospel to every creature' (Mark 16:15; Matthew 28:18–20).

For Pugh this included the masses of people in Wales who were ignorant of the gospel. Constrained therefore by Christ's love, he knew that 'faith comes by hearing, and hearing by the word of God' (Romans 10:17).

The new industrialised areas of South Wales drew Pugh like a magnet because of the vast numbers of men and their families who had relocated for the purpose of employment and who were nearly all ignorant of the gospel. Pugh's passion was to preach Christ anywhere: 'Christ for all', he insisted, 'and all for Christ.' His early vision of 'Cardiff for Christ' was soon enlarged to 'Wales For Christ' when the Forward Movement was recognised by his denomination. He could not resist invitations to preach Christ and hold regular mission meetings. His call to preach the gospel and his appreciation of Calvary were reinforced by the knowledge that the Head of the church had commissioned churches to preach the gospel to everyone. The purpose of his numerous trips to Scotland was to engage in preaching alongside his close friend the Rev. William Ross, and when he holidayed in South Africa, most of the time he spent preaching the gospel as he recognised the desperate spiritual and social needs there, even among Welsh immigrants.

Seth Joshua was asked concerning his experience in working 'before and after the death of John Pugh'. Seth's answer reveals the sense of urgency felt by Pugh:

> There is the greatest possible difference. In John Pugh's day the bugle was always sounding *'The charge'*. The command was *'Up and at them'*. *'Charge'* ... It was an offensive, an attack, a rush to obtain an object. The enemy was kept on the alert ... After John Pugh's day the command was *'Mark Time'* ... The army was kept marking time on the parade ground, close to the canteen...[1]

With the Great Commission ringing in his ears, his heart burning with Calvary love for people and the appalling needs of those living in the industrialised areas of Wales, Pugh was constrained in love to reach out to as many people as possible with the gospel.

- Read and then reflect on the Lord's Great Commission in Matthew 28:18–20 and Mark 16:15.
- In what ways are you involved in reaching unbelievers with the gospel?

2. The Holy Spirit works in varying degrees of power when Christ is preached

When John Pugh preached for a week in Rhyl in special evangelistic meetings in 1891, thirteen years before the 1904–05 revival, we read

> There was an unction and a power about the meetings which was manifestly from on high ... There are not a few who have been greatly blessed. The messages were clear, direct and powerful.[2]

---

1 *Seth and Frank Joshua*, pp. 113–114.
2 *The Christian Standard*, Vol. 1, No. 7, January 1892, p. 12.

Chapter 19

Preaching in Llanidloes, mid-Wales, over a few days many were converted and encouraged under Pugh's Christ-centred ministry with the claim made:

Never was there more powerful preaching.[3]

Similarly preaching in Oswestry for several days of evangelistic meetings (1892), the church reported

Mr Pugh's preaching was very powerful and impressive.[4]

The same year, John Pugh returned to his first pastorate in Tredegar to preach in a five-day mission marking twenty years since he was first inducted there as pastor in 1872. More people were saved during these 1892 meetings and the church was greatly encouraged. Under Pugh's successor, the Lord continued to add to the church by conversions of unchurched people.

John Pugh reflected on his ministry in Tredegar, outlining how the Lord worked in those earlier years. He had started in his first pastorate as a 'raw student' and only four years old as a Christian. Their first building was a small iron building erected on a cinder tip which soon became too small:

The Lord was present with us in the New Chapel as in the Iron Chapel and a strong church ... was built up to the glory of the Redeemer and in praise of the gospel for Mr Pugh determined not to know anything save Jesus Christ and Him crucified. Mr Pugh has no faith in anything, save in personal contact with the personal Saviour. This he feels is the one need of sinners, and anything short of this ... is only patchwork ... Some hundreds were gathered into the various churches through his open-air services in nine years and his own church was receiving some additions continually ...[5]

---

3 *The Christian Standard*, Vol. 1, No. 9, March 1892, pp. 8–9.
4 *The Christian Standard*, Vol. 1, No. 12, June 1892, p. 10.
5 *The Christian Standard*, Vol. 2, No. 16, November 1892, p. 7.

The above examples are a small sample of responses from those who heard Pugh preach, illustrating the unusual and varying degrees of power given him in declaring Christ crucified.

The same is true of Pugh's colleagues like Seth Joshua, H. G. Howell and Jonny Ray.

Mardy Rees,[6] for example, reports that 1903 was 'one of the most remarkable' periods in Seth Joshua's ministry when 'conversions took place constantly at his meetings and as many as fifty were brought to Christ in one church' alone. Earlier, in August 1895, Seth began mission work in Newport[7] and hired the Temperance Hall where 'many conversions took place ... The congregations became so large that overflow meetings were held in the Corn Exchange' and when these services ended, another service started almost immediately for those standing idly on the streets. At the end of the first year, at least one hundred people professed conversion and were constituted into a church!

Or think of H. G. Howell who had worked as an evangelist in London and North Wales. Aware that the Lord had led him significantly, Pugh invited him to Cardiff to assume responsibility for the new work in East Moors and Pugh writes that he 'began his glorious ministry in July 1891'.[8] During his ministry there and later in Monthemer Road Hall, 'many hundreds were brought to the Saviour'. This was a regular feature of the ministries of the evangelists over the preceding decade and prior to the national revival of 1904–05, a revival they also prayed and longed for!

- Are you praying for the Holy Spirit to make gospel preaching and personal evangelism more effective?

- In what way is the Lord working in your situation?

---

6 *Seth and Frank Joshua*, p. 61.
7 *Seth and Frank Joshua*, pp. 112–113.
8 *Grace, Grit & Gumption*, p. 67.

3. Pugh and his colleagues prayed for God to empower the Word preached

Pugh and his colleagues depended on the Lord to give power in preaching, otherwise they knew no one would be saved. 'Salvation is of the Lord' (Jonah 2:9).

To describe Pugh as 'a prayer-warrior, especially in intercessory prayer for the salvation of souls', is accurate, for

Frequently his prayer was the means of conversions. And at more than one open-air meeting, his prayer checked threatened violence or silenced a crude interruption.[9]

Prayer for Pugh and his colleagues was central in their lives and work. Seth Joshua expressed dependence on God by devoting himself to prayer. While evangelising with his brother Frank in Neath, Seth referred often in his diary to times of prayer:

We spent a precious time in prayer today... (1887); we all agreed to lay hold of God for blessing on Neath. My soul is much exercised... (1889); after all had retired to rest, I was compelled to stay up and wrestle in prayer...

Seth 'enjoyed a blessed time of reading and prayer in Sophia Field under a tree. Being

wet there were no people to disturb my meditations...[10]

and often in Sophia Field and alongside the river, Seth enjoyed precious times of prayer.

Prayer for these men held a central place in their lives as they depended on the Lord to make their preaching fruitful.

- What can we learn about prayer from these men?

---

9 *Grace, Grit & Gumption*, p. 160.
10 *Seth and Frank Joshua*, pp. 47, 68.

- Why are prayer and dependence on God inseparably related?

4. Pugh's ministry and revival

The following points are basic in understanding the nature of revival and Pugh's ministry:

- Revival should not be confused with missions or evangelistic activity.
- Nor is revival something Christians can obtain any time they want. Revival is given by God when, where and how He pleases.
- Nor do excitement or physical manifestations belong to the *essence* of revival.
- Church growth often occurs outside periods of revival and the two should not be confused, although on occasions church growth can merge into a localised revival.
- Revival differs from the 'ordinary' work of the Holy Spirit *only* in that it involves greater degrees of the Holy Spirit's power upon the Word, making the Lord's presence more real and awesome, while giving irresistible power to the Word being preached resulting in many conversions and the quickening of the church within a brief period of time.
- Christ is always glorified in such powerful movements of the Spirit.
- Preaching Christ crucified is vital because the Spirit's chief work is to glorify Christ (John 16:14).
- Although there are varying degrees of power in the Holy Spirit's ministry, the church or the individual believer are never without the Holy Spirit. The Holy Spirit is constantly working.
- While gospel preaching may appear ineffective, yet the Holy Spirit blesses the message in various ways; sometimes only much later will a preacher hear of conversions resulting from his preaching.

20. Word and Spirit (2)

In order to clarify further whether revival occurred during Pugh's ministry, we now use a question and answer format in this chapter to pursue the subject further:

Q1: *Did Pugh and his evangelists experience revival in their ministries prior to the 1904–05 revival?*
A: The rate at which new churches were planted in industrial areas in South Wales between 1870 and 1900 was remarkable. One only needs to think of the East Moors Centre, a work initiated by Pugh and Seth Joshua in May 1891 so that by the Spring of 1892 *The Christian Standard*[1] reported

Attendances have been considerable and spiritual results have been most gratifying. On Sunday 17 April 1892 ... 16 converts were received into fellowship ... our church, comprising over 70 members, is entirely made up, with the exception of only four or five, of recent converts brought in from the world...

And this was a frequent occurrence with many people trusting Christ under gospel preaching in the open air or in temporary or permanent buildings. Here was church growth on a scale not known in Wales for decades:

The work accomplished during the last eighteen months, and still going on, in Cardiff, Rhondda and the Valleys of Monmouthshire, is simply wonderful.[2]

Surprisingly, in the summer of 1905, Pugh referred to

---
1 Vol. 1, No. 11, May 1892, pp. 4–5.
2 *The Christian Standard*, Vol. 2, No. 18, January 1893, p. 5.

the glorious revival with which our land has been favoured and which, as a (Forward) Movement, we have been experiencing *for the past fourteen years* [italics mine]. We rejoice that the people of God throughout the Principality have participated in this glorious revival.[3]

Pugh was clearly delighted with what the Lord did prior to 1904–05 and twice in the above quotation describes this 'revival' as being 'glorious', and experienced throughout Wales. Notice the claim that the Forward Movement had been experiencing revival 'for the past fourteen years' is one we can agree with.

Q2: *Were churches praying for revival during this period?*
A: Certainly some churches were praying for revival and they were encouraged to do so.

The General Assembly of the Presbyterian Church of Wales called all its local churches to hold a week of prayer for revival in January 1893:

…that we may have the power of the Holy Spirit upon us all as in the days of old when Howel Harris carried with him wherever he went the power of God … Never was there a greater need than now. Never was there possibly such a longing for it. Never were there more numerous … pleadings for an overwhelming power than now.

Another example is an address given to students at Trefeca College by Professor Powell, Cardiff, who gave a layman's perspective of the spiritual condition of the denomination and urged students to pray for a much-needed revival because:

…the state of things is not so satisfactory … now there is less individual conviction and spiritual apprehension … the churches of the past generation were filled with people to whom conversion was a reality… they had seen great things and experienced great things and knew in Whom they believed. Now another generation has arisen which

---

3 *The Forward Movement Magazine*, September 1905, p. 41.

Chapter 20

has not seen the great work of God ... we now have vague questioning, uncertainty and unrest ...[4]

Q3: *Returning to a previous question, was revival therefore experienced during Pugh's ministry, prior to the 1904–05 revival?*
A: In January 1905, *The Monthly Treasury* carried the exciting news:

All our readers will have heard that in some parts of South Wales a very gracious spiritual awakening is now in progress. Our God, our covenant God, has remembered us and is doing great things for us. For some years we have been endeavouring to solve the problem of the lapsed masses ... Pastors and deacons have been at their wits' ends to know how to win the people ... we have tried social gatherings, choirs, guilds, missions and societies, various amusements, yet the crowds did not come ... But our God has come and lo! In less than a month the problem is being solved ... chapels are crowded, prayer meetings are more popular than football matches, and sinners are being swept into salvation.

Thus we are rebuked ... and reminded that the church is spiritual ... Let us humble ourselves before God. Let us confess our iniquity ... There is another side to it ... Amid all the difficulties of the past, there has been faithful preaching of the old gospel ... teaching in Sunday Schools ... and the church has not been without a remnant and now this is bearing fruit ... Take heart ...

However, as we have noticed, long before 1904–05, there were remarkable results following the preaching of Pugh and his evangelists, and this over several years with large numbers saved in different places and new churches established. Their ministries stood out, so Pugh's claim they had revival during their ministries is credible.

The answer to the question is that revivals can be localised in one church or area whereas the 1904–05 revival was national rather than localised. Apart from Pugh and his colleagues, there were numerous local revivals in Tredegar (1866), Newport and Cardiff (1871), Carmarthen and

---

4 *The Monthly Treasury*, Vol. 1 (NS), No. 9, September 1900, pp. 4–8.

Blaenau Ffestiniog (1878). When the Rev. Richard Owen died in 1887, his brief ministry among the Presbyterians in North West Wales resulted in about 13,000 people being converted. Similarly, John Pugh and colleagues saw many people turn to Christ as a result of their preaching. Historically, small localised revivals occurred regularly in different places but the 1904–05 revival was more extensive and national.[5]

Q4: *Did concern over the spiritual condition of churches and the spiritual needs of the country prompt prayer for revival?*
A: Yes. For example, the Rev. John Hughes wrote three articles on the Person and Work of the Holy Spirit in which he lamented that:

> We have too little communion with Him and do not often enough open our hearts to His power and His love; the consequence is that our work and life bear too little the impress of being His work. Let us lift up our hearts to God in prayer…[6]

More often the need for revival was felt more keenly with regard to preaching, as when Dr Cynddylan Jones explained that the great need of preachers is spiritual power involving believing and studying God's Word but also believing in the Spirit of God. He warned preachers:

> Truth alone and by itself, though divine truth, cannot conquer the will and regenerate the heart. Having prepared our best sermons, we must then bow the knee and pray the Holy Spirit to vitalise the truth and make it instrumental to save the soul. Like Elijah, we should carefully gather together the fuel, and lay the sacrifice on the altar and then with Elijah say, 'Oh God, send the fire, send the fire.'[7]

Others, like the Rev. Richard Morgan, wrote about the need for revival, explaining that

---

5 Details of some localised revivals are provided by Eifion Evans in his book, *The Welsh Revival of 1904* (Bangor, Evangelical Movement of Wales, 1969), especially pp. 9–27.
6 *The Christian Standard*, Vol. 2, No. 19, February 1893, pp. 4–5.
7 *The Monthly Treasury*, Vol. 2, No. 23, November 1895, p. 19.

Chapter 20

the history of the church shows it has its times and seasons, periods of depression, prosperity ... there are also times when its life breaks forth in fruitful seasons and bountiful harvests, times of refreshing from the presence of the Lord.

He then made three points of application. First, 'true revivalists always have been men of faith'; but secondly he emphasised that 'revivals are always carried on by means of personal influence when the gospel becomes a reality and the heart is filled with love for Christ and s/he becomes a living power and influence'. Thirdly, 'churches should always be anxiously awaiting the coming of the Lord in His Spirit to revive His work in the hearts of people but not to incite and bring in strange fire'.[8]

A significant number of believers and congregation had recognised the urgent need for greater degrees of the Spirit's power in the life and witness of their churches. Their prayers were partially answered in numerous localised revivals such as those under Pugh's ministry.

Q5: *Did Christians agree at the time concerning the nature of revival and the means of obtaining it?*
A: Theologically the situation was complex, for in the late nineteenth-century, the biblical and reformed understanding of the Holy Spirit's work was being denied by liberal teaching or subtly modified by 'Holiness' and 'Keswick' teachings.

The Monthly Treasury[9] reported on the 1894 Keswick Convention in England[10] which 12–15 people from Wales had attended. The object of the Convention was 'the deepening of the spiritual life', encouraging 'out-and-out surrender to Christ and being better fitted to serve the Lord'. While being supportive of the Convention, the report referred to 'much prejudice' against its teaching. But why go to the Keswick Convention? The answer given was: 'It makes doctrine more experiential.' In 1903 the first Keswick-in-Wales Convention was held in Llandrindod Wells and Seth Joshua attended. He reported:

---

8 *The Christian Standard*, Vol. 2, No. 21, April 1893, pp. 3–5.
9 Vol. 1, No. 11, November 1894, pp. 7–10.
10 Founded in 1875 by the vicar of St John's Church in Keswick who had served there for 32 years.

Word and Spirit (2)

I received a definite spiritual blessing at Llandrindod. My heart had been prepared for this by deep trial and experience.[11]

Many, like Dr Joseph Jenkins, Newquay, also received blessing from its teaching, but others like Seth Joshua became uneasy concerning its message, especially in its being 'too dogmatic'.[12]

Eifion Evans is correct in describing the church as being 'doctrinally off balance' when the 1904–05 revival commenced, and then the lack of teaching and preaching[13] during and following the revival aggravated the problem.[14] Key terms like regeneration, sanctification/holiness and baptism with the Holy Spirit were modified but in ways not always recognised as being off-centre biblically.

Q6: *What are the main lessons to learn from John Pugh regarding the Word-Spirit relationship?*
A: Pugh's major focus was on the Lord, His glorious gospel, the appalling spiritual needs of the masses of people in the country and the necessity of the Spirit of God to change the hearts and lives of sinners under the preaching of Christ. These were his major concerns and prayer therefore was at the heart of his evangelism. God's gospel was all-important for him and he longed that all the people should hear this good news and trust Christ. For that reason he trusted God's Spirit to use the gospel powerfully whether in or out of revival for conversions and for the quickening of Christ's church. Pugh and his fellow-evangelists were privileged to know greater degrees of the Spirit's power in their preaching, but they knew that success was due entirely to the Lord.

---

11 *Seth and Frank Joshua*, pp. 61, 68–69.
12 After attending the Keswick-in-Wales Convention in 1904, he wrote: the Keswick teaching is 'too dogmatic with regard to the steps leading into the blessing of spiritual fullness. My opinion is that the land of milk and honey is reached by many separate paths, and that the Holy Spirit leads into this in His own way ... preach the Truth and leave it to God's Spirit'.
13 I have described and assessed the theological differences in Wales during this period between Reformed theology and the 'Holiness'/Keswick teachings in Welsh in 'Sancteiddrwydd a'r Diwygiad', pp. 146–156 in *NEFOL DAN: Agweddau ar Ddiwygiad 1904–05*, Noel Gibbard, Golygydd, (Pen-y-bont ar Ogwr, Gwasg Bryntirion, 2004).
14 *The Welsh Revival of 1904*, pp. 9–27.

Chapter 20

These are among the major challenges for our churches in the twenty-first century.

In the next and final chapter, we offer some practical insights regarding the situation in which Pugh exercised his ministry, insights which encourage us in serving the Lord in our post-Christian contemporary society.

21. Contemporary challenges

This final chapter is different. First, the chapter begins by underlining the importance and centrality of God's Word. John Pugh treasured the Bible as God's supremely authoritative revelation of Himself and His purpose and we must do the same today whether we are discouraged or encouraged in the Lord's work. The first part of this chapter illustrates the early influence of the Bible which led eventually to Pugh's conversion. Secondly, three quotations are provided, two of which relate to revival but in a challenging and exciting manner, and then the final quotation illustrates care and support for pastors. John Pugh cared about pastors and was concerned that they were appreciated, supported both prayerfully and practically by their congregations. Pugh also expressed understanding for the needs of his evangelists, and the final quotation therefore is one which Pugh would endorse wholeheartedly. Pastors need to be loved and prayed for by their congregations!

A. God's Word

'So shall My word be that goes forth from My mouth; it shall not return to Me empty, but it shall accomplish what I please, and it shall prosper in the thing for which I sent it' (Isaiah 55:11).

The sowing and watering of God's Word will never be wasted even though we may not often be aware how God uses it and gives the increase (1 Corinthians 3:6–7). After describing how Pugh's preaching was used by the Lord, you may be discouraged in thinking of your own local church where there is little or no church growth. To encourage you, I remind you of the way in which John Pugh became a Christian and the role of God's Word in his early life.

Chapter 21

Looking more closely at the way John Pugh came to Christ, there are several important links in the chain. Importantly, he had Christian parents who loved the Lord and were faithful as a family in attending church meetings. We must never underestimate the value of a godly, prayerful Christian home and family worship. John also attended the local church with his parents regularly and heard the gospel preached there. There were Christian relatives too, including an aunt who made John promise to read the Bible daily as he left with his parents to go to Pembrokeshire at the age of fourteen. This background and grounding in God's Word was hugely significant in preparation for his conversion which did not occur in a vacuum.

In leaving mid-Wales and its more sheltered life, the fourteen-year-old boy was excited as he began secular work for his father but soon he was influenced by ungodly labourers for whom drinking alcohol was their favourite pastime. He found this appealing and soon began to drink with them in their leisure periods, a fact he was later ashamed of.

In the Lord's providence, Ezra Roberts, a business partner with John's father, had been praying for these unchurched labourers and was eager for them to hear the gospel of Christ. As a prominent member of the Calvinistic Methodist church in Wales, he knew of young men training for the Christian ministry who could serve as chaplains to these labourers during their long summer vacations. The Lord's blessing was on the venture and two students were influential in preparing further for John Pugh's conversion, namely, David Lloyd Jones and T. Charles Edwards. Their friendship was valued by Pugh, while their preaching was also used powerfully in his life. In the background, we need to remember his promise to a relative to read the Bible regularly which he did, and sometimes he was challenged by what he read.

CLIMAX

The climax came one Sunday when it rained heavily throughout the day so that the family were unable to walk to their church some distance away. To pass the time at home but especially in concern for his spiritual condition, John's mother gave him the latest copy of the Welsh Calvinistic

Contemporary challenges

Methodist magazine Y *Drysorfa* to read. John read the magazine and found it interesting, but a sermon on Revelation 1:17–18 was used to bring him under conviction of sin. He trembled as he read and re-read the sermon, recognising that he was a guilty sinner before a holy God. Almost immediately he felt compelled to go to his knees and beg forgiveness from God and to trust Christ. He was now a Christian and a changed person. The prayers of relatives and friends for his conversion were now answered!

These details are a reminder today of the strategic importance of quality friendships, godly parents, family worship, prayer, reading Christian literature and the regular use of the means of grace such as the preaching of God's Word. God's Word is 'living and powerful' (Hebrews 4:12) and accomplishes God's purpose in the Lord's time.

- Despite our busy lives today, are we diligent in private/family prayer and attending preaching services?
- Christian relatives and friends can be important links in an individual, whether young or old, becoming a Christian.
- Do you recognise the supreme importance and role of God's Word in people becoming Christians?

B. The Holy Spirit—'the heart of the church'

The Rev. John Hughes, Liverpool, at the Conference of North Wales English Presbyterian Churches meeting at Menai Bridge in 1891, provided a biblical overview of the Person and Work of the Holy Spirit with bold pastoral application to churches. The following extract provides food for thought:

Christ is the head of the church … and the Holy Spirit is the *heart* of the church, so the health and soundness of the church and its capacity for work depend on it being full of the Spirit. And is it not a fact that many of our churches in these days are suffering from **heart disease**? … Many profess Christianity who take no delight in Christ (Colossians 2:19). How can they hold to the Head, when they have not been united to Him by the Spirit of the living God? Is there in us … a constant and a deep

Chapter 21

conviction in these days of the need of the Holy Spirit and of our dependence upon Him in our work as ministers and as office-bearers in the church?[1]

Hughes then presented a strong rebuke and reminder to churches:

… it is feared we are content to do many things in our days without the Spirit; but we cannot save a single soul, we cannot comfort a single saint, we cannot bring a single mite into the treasury … without the presence of the Holy Spirit … whenever there has been a moving of the dead bones and a quickening of men's souls, and a time of refreshing in the church of Christ, it has been owing to the work of the Holy Spirit.

John Pugh would have endorsed these words heartily!

- Are we suffering from *'heart disease'*?
- How will we respond to this quotation personally and corporately?

C. Machynlleth, Gwynedd: *'we experienced a revival'* (1888)

I love reading this account of a local revival as it is so refreshing in describing how a small fellowship without famous preachers turned to the Lord and experienced a powerful movement of the Spirit. John Pugh had preached here on a couple of occasions, but the blessing was sovereignly given to this small group of believers and cannot be traced to any one preacher. Be encouraged!

'Poplar Square' was a 'beautiful little mission room in the small town of Machynlleth' founded in 1876 by a devoted servant of Christ, the late Rev. John Foulkes Jones.

In 1888 'we experienced a revival—Jesus Himself drew near and set our hearts aglow with fresh love for Him and for people. One Sunday evening after the service over twelve of us remained for an after-meeting and under a deep feeling of our unworthiness, opened our hearts before God, surrendering ourselves there and then to His service, praying He might use us—He in His mercy smiled upon us.

---

1 *The Christian Standard*, Vol. 2, No. 18, January 1893, p. 4.

Contemporary challenges

From that moment, the little Mission has gone through a period of aggressive work hitherto unknown in our midst. We drew no plans, but from that Sabbath in September 1888, the few members at Poplar are different, the meetings are different; 'all things are new'; 'a flood of light and love entered our souls'; 'His Word in our hearts is like a burning fire'; meetings grew in numbers and intensity ... the workers met together for praise and prayer instead of talking about 'the cause' ... Oh that we were more like Him in everything.

We shall ever praise Him for all he has done for us: 'Not unto us, O Lord, not unto us, but unto Thy Name be the glory' ... Cottage prayer meetings are multiplied. Occasionally we venture to hold an 'open-air' ... The Bible seemed new to us and we began to see that 'the promise was unto us' ... we became conscious of being used—owned by our blessed Master. We have had discouragements and frowns from many a quarter, but He ever smiles and says, 'I am with you always' (Matthew 28:19–20).

The small fellowship was led to hold services in a 'Common Lodging House' every Sunday evening and some weeknights:

These are times of refreshing to our souls and oh! How glorious the gospel is when brought into contact with ... publicans and sinners, the fallen, the degraded, the tramps—the lost sheep are there, the lost piece of silver and we have found prodigals there every Sunday. May the Lord of the harvest pardon our slothfulness over the years when we sat in chapel ... and never thought of the poor perishing souls we should be rescuing ...

The Lord led the small church in other ways too:

Encouraged, we were led into 'the highways and hedges' and to an area called 'the park' where there were caravans, travelling hawkers, show people, tinkers ... for these Jesus died and His love constrained us to go after them whenever we have opportunity ... they cannot read ...

A final exhortation was given to readers by Hugh Davies, the author of this report:

Chapter 21

The ordained ministry is never going to do all the work. Let us lay ourselves on the altar and go forth in simple dependence upon His help and without a shadow of a doubt God's purpose shall be accomplished.

The gospel of the Blessed God is entrusted to us. It needs no subtlety, no splendid skill. It asks only wholehearted obedience and the blessing of God must come. God grant that the latent forces of our community may hear the cry of the lonely hearts and the weary souls who perish at their very doors.[2]

- What interests you concerning this account of the movement of the Holy Spirit?
- Is there one aspect of this account which encourages and/or stands out for you?

D. 'Pastor's Help League'

One church deacon

'wondered how he could encourage his pastor who carried a considerable workload. He decided to get others to help and he formed a Pastor's Help League' (PHL) and with two members to start. No announcement was made to the church. The church was to know as little as possible. The pastor knew nothing of it. The PHL was to grow cautiously and with no special meetings.

They decided to start for one month and agreed on five points:

1. They would pray twice daily for the pastor. This was the most important aspect.
2. They would be in church five minutes before the service started in order to pray for the pastor.
3. Attend the weekly church prayer meeting regularly.
4. Double their contribution to the Ministry Fund.
5. Present pastor now and then with a book.

---

2 *The Christian Standard*, Vol. 1, No. 10, April 1892, pp. 3–6.

Contemporary challenges

One further member was added at the end of the first month.[3]

They wanted to grow so they prayed about having a fourth member. The pastor was glad to see them in the church prayer meeting and the deacons noticed an increase in giving on Sundays. Pastor told the deacons they should **all** be in the prayer meeting regularly ... Some deacons felt guilty. In the next prayer meeting all the deacons were present—something unknown in the church for many years.

When the four members of the PHL met next, they were aware of a young man who had been attending the church prayer meeting without being in their PHL. His name was approved by them to join and when he was told, he wept, saying that over the past three to four weeks he had felt moved towards the pastor and the church and longed to help. He too joined the Pastor's Help League.

The initiative of the three young men has served to revive the church in an extraordinary way. The pastor has been heartened considerably, the deacons are new men, the prayer meetings have grown and church growth is continuing ... GOD HEARS PRAYER![4]

An imaginary story? Not really. Why are you surprised? This is what the Lord can do through His people, even through one or two believers!

- What is your reaction to the initiative taken by one deacon?
- How can we personally support our local church pastors and leaders spiritually and practically?

Conclusion

Thank you for reading this biography of John Pugh which is intended as a basic introduction to his life and work. In 1896, one article in *The Monthly Treasury* claimed:

---

3 *The Monthly Treasury*, Vol. VII, No. 5, May 1906, pp 3–4.
4 *The Monthly Treasury*, Vol. 7, No. 7, July 1906, pp. 3–4.

Chapter 21

Everybody in Wales has heard of John Pugh ... everybody is acquainted with his powerful voice. Everybody admits the warmth of his heart ... and are intimate with his gigantic projects and his Forward Movement and Church Extension schemes...

In the twenty-first century, sadly, very few people know about John Pugh, and that is the reason why the book has been written. The purpose, however, is not to praise the man himself, for he had his faults, but rather to acknowledge God's grace in his life and how the Lord equipped him by the Holy Spirit to preach Christ and Him crucified powerfully and fruitfully.

May the Lord quicken us all in our respective situations and give us such a love of the Lord and of people that we too will witness the Lord rebuilding and extending His church again by the Holy Spirit. He is able!